To
Winnie and Hannah
&
Raffael, JJ, Lina and Do

Women
Leading the Way in
Brussels

Claudia de Castro Caldeirinha
Corinna Hörst

 JOHN HARPER PUBLISHING

Women Leading the Way in Brussels
ISBN 978-0-9934549-9-8

John Harper Publishing, London
www.johnharperpublishing.co.uk

Design and typeset by Simone Meesters, the Netherlands
Printed and bound by Gutenberg Press Ltd, Malta

Table of Contents

PART III: REFLECTIONS AND CONCLUSIONS

PART IV: RESOURCES FOR CHANGE-MAKERS

Acknowledgements

Embarking on this book led to a long, but fun and enriching journey. We grew closer as friends, partners and colleagues as we worked together and came to truly appreciate our complementary approaches to the topics we were covering. We also met some incredible people along the way who helped us on our journey. Their support, time, feedback, expertise, insights, criticism, questions, comments, edits and assistance were invaluable.

First of all, we would like to thank the 14 fantastic women who agreed to embark with us on this adventure and who were willing to share their stories. Meeting them and working with them was astonishing, and we could have sat forever listening to their personal stories and experiences. Without them, this book would not exist!

We are grateful to John Harper for his trust, encouragement and faith in the idea behind this book. His advice, perspectives and British pragmatism throughout the process were precious, and his patience with delayed draft submissions fabulous!

We would like to especially thank Bela Kapur whose directness and honesty about our arguments and writing made us cringe at times, yet forced us to really make our case and hone our language. We would also like to thank Julia Stamm who was there with us when we conceived the book, whose scientific eye aided us in creating the questionnaire and who then became our first peer reviewer. Marion Sharples, as an English native speaker, representative of a different generation and well versed in gender studies helped us enormously with the editing process.

The help of our amazing assistants and interns was crucial in staying on track and managing the many aspects of getting a book done: Paulina Ek, Veronica Francis, Laura Gronendaal, Alazne Irigoien, Pavlina Markopoulou, Tatiana Morales, Ediz Rehberg, Lucy Right and Emma Tulley. Their presence kept us on our toes and, as younger women and men eager to make their way in the world, they were a constant reminder as to why we decided to write this book. And a particular big thank you to Jean-Jacques Quinet and his Studio 5 sur 5 for all the help in setting up and recording the interviews!

There were many other wonderful people who were there for us, men and women who shared their perspectives from their respective professional fields and gave feedback and suggestions. We are particularly thankful, among others, to Irune Aguirrezabal, Elke Anklam, Rosa Balfour, Ilze Baltmane, Daniela Bankier, Paloma Castro, Christine Cecil, Claire Craanen, Marion Debruyne, Kristin Engvig, Sabine Henzler, Agnes Hubert, Thinam Jakobs, Monika Ladmanova, Marta Martinelli, Pauline Massart, Joanna Maycock, Silvana Koch-Mehrin, Penny Naas, Petra Pinzler, Francesca Ratti, Claudia Ritter, Christine Roger, Tamara Sanne, Friederike Tschampa, Emma Udwin and Ana Yturriaga. Their insights from their particular professional fields and personal experiences of living and working in Brussels have influenced the content of the book.

We are also grateful to the men who agreed to be part of our project, replied to our survey and/or gave input and support through the different phases of our work. We would particularly like to thank Ira Chaleff, Ryan Heath, Ian Lesser, John Richardson, Gerry Salole, Bruno van Pottelsberghe, Sir Graham Watson and Marc Wilikens, who each provided ideas, important insights and new perspectives, and at times challenged our assumptions and continued to press us to write in a more inclusive way.

And finally, we would like to thank those who sustained us throughout the project at a personal level. Our partners, Jean-Jacques and Mohamed, for their patience, kindness and the fact of being there – notwithstanding the ups and downs of the "creative process". Our children – for being tough critics and creative advisors – or simply as a reminder that the future must promise more equitable options for girls and boys, in Europe and elsewhere. And there is also a large "thanks" to our families, who raised us, shaped us, challenged us, and enabled us as best they could, and in the end helped us become who we are today.

Many others have also generously provided inspiration, time, advice and criticism, and are not mentioned here. We are grateful to be part of amazing communities in Brussels and to know that there is work ongoing that complements what this book is trying to achieve: to put women firmly, visibly and proudly on the map in Brussels – and Europe.

As we spoke to people from all over Europe, the recurring question was: "How is the book going? And when will it be out?" Well, here it is – may it inspire others (you) to tell your story, to serve as role models, to lead towards positive change, and to help define what it means to exercise leadership on your own terms!

The Authors

Claudia de Castro Caldeirinha

Claudia is the founder and Executive Director of RedScope Consulting (www.redscope-consulting.com) and had the original idea for this book. She started her academic career writing a Master's thesis on "Gender Identity through Conflict situations" and, over time, she has mainstreamed gender in her diverse professional challenges, all over the world. Today, Claudia is a senior practitioner combining international relations, leadership development and gender studies. She thrives on two approaches: bringing different people together to create unconventional solutions; and assisting people and organisations to develop (innovative and ethical) strategies that respond to our challenges today. She works in Brussels and globally to advance a value-driven community of change-makers: Leadership professionals, academics and practitioners. Among the many initiatives, she leads the incipient Trans-Atlantic Women in Leadership Forum, jointly with key actors from Europe and the USA. Claudia is an active member of the International Leadership Association.

Born in East Timor, Claudia has witnessed how women are often the major victims of conflict and yet how, paradoxically, they are also the backbone of resilience, social organisation and resistance. This experience triggered an early political conscience and a profound determination to promote freedom, democracy and human rights.

Today, Claudia's life mission is to contribute to a more democratic Europe and world and to help build inclusive societies where both men and women can fully contribute with their talents and skills. In addition to running RedScope Consulting, she teaches at universities, is a senior leadership advisor to EU institutions and international, private and non-governmental organisations, and is an active public speaker. Claudia is a certified coach of leaders and leaders-to-be, a mentor, and an engaged citizen, active in multiple pro-democracy forums, activities and publications. She is also the mother of a young boy who defines himself as a feminist!

Dr. Corinna Hörst

Corinna is Deputy Director of the Brussels office of the German Marshall Fund of the US (GMF) and a Senior Fellow. She is also the president of Women in International Security (WIIS) in Brussels. In addition, Corinna founded the European Network of Female Policy Experts in Brussels with the purpose of promoting and facilitating gender equality in EU policy debates by raising the profile of female policy experts in Brussels through programming, networking and an online platform, the BXL Binder (www.brusselsbinder.org), and thereby adding innovative ideas to the policy debates.

Aside from her transatlantic policy work, Corinna advises on strategic planning, institution-building, operations and staff management, as well as leadership development, including mentoring. Corinna's networks reach into EU institutions, governments, media, business and foundations, as well as non-governmental and think-tank communities, where she often facilitates contact across sectors. Corinna has seen GMF change from a grant-making institution, to an operational foundation, to a public policy institution and think-tank. This experience has enabled her to learn about change management – experiencing, first hand, the challenges involved in being sensitive to diversity.

Corinna describes herself as an international relations junkie and very lucky to have lived on both sides of the Atlantic. She combines her "Europeanness" and appreciation for historical contexts with an American entrepreneurial spirit and can-do attitude. But an American lens does not always fit in Europe and she has come to develop a consciousness of European styles of working, interacting and leading. The absence of stringent cultural norms in the unique setting of Brussels has enabled Corinna to be a single parent by choice, working full time. In the past, when she did not travel for work, she used to explore Belgium and beyond by motorcycle, which gave her an unfiltered view of countries, societies and people. She is guided by a deep sense of justice, loyalty and an appreciation for intellectual diversity. She is the mother of a girl who reminds Corinna every day of the reason why she is passionate about these principles.

Introduction

"Ensuring that women are able to reach the highest levels of leadership and responsibility is important for humanity and economics."
Christine Lagarde

"In a society where the rights and potential of women are constrained, no man can be truly free. He may have power, but he will not have freedom."
Mary Robinson

In 2001 a young Portuguese woman arrived in Brussels by motorbike, coming from Rome amidst one of the biggest floods ever in North Italy and Switzerland. She came, as so many others do, to start a traineeship in the European Commission, whilst concluding her PhD studies at the European University Institute. Her intention was to stay in town for a year and to then proceed to a sunnier place for a career with the United Nations. Challenges succeeded opportunities… professional endeavours followed other professional projects… friends left and new friends were made, and a child was born. Time passed, and she remained seduced by this grey city that hosts the heart of Europe.

In the fall of 2002, a German woman arrived from the United States and checked herself into a hotel. She was to begin a new job in the recently opened Brussels office of her American organisation. So far, she had not really focused much on European affairs and only knew a few people in town. Her role was to connect the new office with headquarters, establish structures for transatlantic programmes and help bring US voices to town. She was still drawn to the entrepreneurial spirit of the US but was also longing to reconnect with her roots in Europe, having lived away from her home continent for 10 years. She fell in love with Brussels on second sight, made friends, settled down in her ways and had a child on her own.

We, Claudia and Corinna, were these two young women.

When we arrived in Brussels, we missed having a "guide" to help us understand the dynamics that define and shape much of the city. We missed guidance in understanding and navigating our new reality – how the city works, where to get assistance, how to become part of relevant professional groups and activities, how to develop and nourish our unique leadership styles, how to operate in this multicultural and multi-sectorial space, both as professionals as well as women.

In fact, as we look back, we didn't even know that we lacked this information. We didn't even know these were some of the questions we were going to have to trek through. Instead, it took us years to observe, learn and understand the dynamics around town. It took us time to realise that one of the big pieces missing from the jigsaw was the stories and experiences of the women who had come before us. It took us years to realise that many other women also missed these role models, their stories, their experiences and lessons. And, perhaps surprisingly, this gap has persisted over time.

one of the big pieces missing was the stories and experiences of the women who had come before us

For more than 15 years, we have had the privilege of meeting and working closely with many of the remarkable women who have been leading the way towards more diverse and inclusive leadership in Europe. Given the invisibility of most of these women and their challenges and achievements, we wanted to make some of their stories visible to a broader audience. And with the European Union enduring trying times, when its rationale and purpose are being questioned, it seemed like an opportune time to reflect not only on its current diversity but also the types of leadership that can contribute to creating new, more inclusive options for Europe's future.

Making Women Visible

By sharing the stories of some notable women, and by sharing our own understanding of Brussels as a distinctive power hub and some of the important experiences, connections and insights we have made in this city, we hope to assist those women who plan to make a career in Brussels. This book is also addressed to those already here who are doing amazing work but who would like to take advantage to the fullest extent of the opportunities provided by this city. In sum, we hope these stories and the women behind them will inspire other women, not simply to copy but to find their own leadership styles – and to make leadership and decision-making more reflective of the Brussels, Europe and world that we aspire to live in: more inclusive, equitable and hopeful.

We also realised that too many opportunities for women's professional development are often invisible or accessible only to a small niche of people. Networks, mentoring programmes, leadership development initiatives, and interesting events around entrepreneurship and career development are emerging, but most remain isolated in silos, within one sector or around a specific group agenda. So initiating a compilation of the increasing opportunities in Brussels to support women's leadership and professional development became a complementary exercise for us.

Filling a Big Gap

We believe that the stories of European women leaders have been largely untold. Unlike American women leaders, who have been more visible in public life – both at home and abroad – European women have been, until recently, reticent about claiming their space at the top.

With this in mind, we have gathered together a collection of personal, frank and revealing vignettes of 14 women, based on our interviews with them, who exercise leadership across different sectors in Brussels. The stories show how it is possible to lead in many different ways and with many diverse strategies.

European women have been reticent about claiming their space at the top

Interestingly, most of our interviewees said that they would not consider themselves leaders and role models. This cautiousness can partially be explained by the complexity of Europe with its different regions and countries, the persistence of patriarchal systems and the multiple national nuances concerning gender roles and policies.

Our book is a first contribution to these important discussions facing our European societies as to how European women experience and exercise leadership. We also share ideas, tips, and concrete advice, both throughout the different stories and in the final sections. Finally, we aim to encourage reflection on what it means to be a woman leader in the heart of Europe today.

Leadership is Personal

This book is a personal and necessarily subjective endeavour. We recognise that we cannot be comprehensive nor universal in our findings. Not every finding will apply to every woman aspiring to lead. We shared our experiences, stories and exchanges – and we have brought in our own networks, contacts, perceptions.

We come from different countries and regions in Europe, where history, opportunities and social patterns are different. We can therefore recognise the circumstances that provide different historical and cultural backgrounds for European women. While all of our interviewees shared with us the view that gender parity is necessary, we became acutely aware of the nuances in perceptions and priorities arising from how women from different parts of Europe see their role in society and their professional advancement. While the stories will show these nuances, we will say more on this topic in the concluding sections.

we became acutely aware of the nuances in perceptions and priorities

The Book Structure Ahead

We start with a "Setting the Scene" PART I, with four short chapters covering Brussels, reflecting on leadership and specifically women's leadership in today's Europe, providing a brief overview of gender statistics in the various professional sectors covered in this book, and asking why change is so slow.

We then have the core of the book, PART II – the stories of 14 women from different professional fields, their accounts of how they got to Brussels and into their senior positions, their take on Brussels and their leadership styles.

PART III has a chapter offering "tips from the top", our takeaways from the 14 stories, looking at what the stories have in common and the differences between them. A second chapter, "Moving Forward" contains our final reflections, based on what we have learnt in the process of writing this book, our professional experiences, and the many conversations we had with multiple inspirational people working in the areas of women's leadership and gender diversity.

PART IV is practice-oriented, containing: (1) recommendations to drive change towards more gender-diverse cultures; (2) a list of Brussels initiatives, networks and organisations supporting women professionals and making them more visible.

The book ends with 2 ANNEXES, providing suggestions for further reading and a glossary of acronyms, concepts and jargon.

PART I

SETTING THE SCENE

An Interconnected Context

These days, it is a challenge to discuss Brussels – and what it stands for, Europe – without lapsing into simplified ideas, banal reiterations or adding to gloomy self-fulfilling prophecies. The very volatility, instability and inter-connectedness of today's world, as well as the internal undercurrents within Europe and the European Union, lend extra relevance to any book on leadership in Brussels.

We believe that leadership – or the lack of it – is at the core of today's challenges and tomorrow's solutions. Leaders with diverse backgrounds, experience, skill sets and expertise who can bring varied perspectives into the European "story" are needed to modernise the value-driven, peaceful and prosperous unity among the current members of the European Union. This diversity is equally crucial to reform and modernise the European institutions, in ways that reflect the reality of the diverse EU population.

Women make up half of the citizens of Europe. By making visible the lives, stories and views of women leaders and highlighting the many ways in which women can and do lead, we wish to contribute to a more inclusive account of Brussels, and to a collective reflection on the importance of embracing women's talent in today's decision-making in and about Europe.

A Different Take on Brussels Today

Brussels has been an international hub situated at a cultural crossroads since the time of the Roman Empire. The openness and diversity resulting from its geographic location is today felt and experienced more strongly than ever. Brussels is a Belgian city but it is also the European Union's de facto capital. It is also the city where the different Belgian linguistic communities (French, Flemish and German) converge with Europeans from the EU's 28 member states, as well as a mosaic of other communities from all over the globe. Since its establishment as an independent kingdom in 1831, Belgium has been a melting pot and modern Brussels is an intersection of many peoples, languages, professional circles – and multiple layers of power.

Brussels as the capital of Europe is peculiar: its "Europeanness" is experienced through the people and the multiple languages spoken rather than its buildings and monuments, which in most of the city have a distinctively Belgian stamp. The city has never truly managed to create a sense of centralised power nor a strong identity as the EU capital – in part because of fear of treading on the sensibilities of the member states.

A core group of international expatriates – or expats – in Brussels are here because of the European Union, or because they represent their governments at other international institutions. Many are either working in the EU institutions or in institutions that engage with the EU in one way or the other: in diplomatic representations, public affairs, advocacy groups, law firms, companies, associations, membership organisations, the World Bank, the North Atlantic Treaty Organisation (NATO), and the United Nations (UN) institutions. Moreover, countries from all over the world commonly have multiple diplomatic representations in Brussels: one to Belgium, a second to the EU and some countries even a third to NATO, which adds to the international character and complexity of layers in the city. Finally, there are those who have come to Brussels attracted by the opportunities that this multicultural space and population provide: entrepreneurs, designers, art dealers, consultants, teachers, and the large number of young people who come to the city as trainees and interns or to start their careers.

All these people co-exist daily in a myriad of spheres of influence and power as well as independence and individuality – many of them remain in their various European "bubbles" and have limited interaction with the Belgian inhabitants. Like in a 3D version of Olympic circles, these groups seem distinctive and restricted entities because of their specific objectives, interest areas, professional and sectorial culture, nationalities – but yet they overlap with others, which means they are inter-connected in complex, rich and multiple ways and cannot exist without one another. Being an individual, a foreigner, or expatriate in Brussels means that you will be part both of your own circle or bubble, and connected to many people – and hence other circles or bubbles.

Brussels is a city that takes time to grow on you. Few people dream of living in Brussels like they would in Paris, London, New York or Prague. The city is primarily associated with bureaucracy due to the presence of the European Union institutions. Many of its working population are transient: Belgians who commute into the city on a daily basis; foreign diplomats on rotation; parliamentarians, staffers, officials and lobbyists who move between Brussels, Strasbourg and Luxembourg. There is the traffic, construction and crime associated with any capital city. Not to mention the grey weather and the long winter season that lends itself easily to newcomers' small talk.

Nonetheless, Brussels is a gem. There is something special about the city and its mix of peoples. While modest and unpretentious, it is a cosmopolitan and international place of politics, business and philanthropy; it is easy to live in, affordable, with ample means of diversion through art, culture, culinary delights, nature as well as access to the rest of Europe. Brussels is also the first major city in Europe in which no nationality and no culture is the absolute majority and the host country does not impose itself on the expats. This creates a space of freedom

the host country does not impose itself on the expats

for foreigners to carve out identities removed from the national norms back home. People can get on together and it is this unobtrusive atmosphere that lets newcomers shape their professional and personal development and succeed. To many who have lived in Brussels, mono-cultural cities can afterwards seem boring, limited and restrictive. Brussels is a strange mixture of Mediterranean laissez-faire and a somewhat Germanic focus on order, process and rules which co-exist in a unique blend. The multiple layers of international circles and groups of influence create multiple centres of power and weight that need each other, yet frequently compete with each other. This book includes the stories of 14 professional women who made the city their own, in these different circles – women who took advantage of what Brussels has to offer and have come to love it.

There are of course other versions of Brussels: a city of poor immigrants, many of them Muslims from North Africa, whose women often experience a very different reality; and a Brussels of the suburbs whose inhabitants have little contact with the "bubble" of cosmopolitan Brussels. Those versions are beyond the scope of this book, which is about Brussels in its role as the EU's capital and an international city.

Women at Work in Brussels

Women are a considerable and steadily expanding part of the international work force in Brussels. They are part of the multiple spheres of influence and power. They are part of specific circles through their professions (for example in the European Commission, or public affairs companies, law firms, international organisations, trade associations or civil society organisations), or because of their nationalities, expertise or specific interests. Yet, like everybody else in this city, they interact and connect with others.

European women today have rights and a degree of financial independence that their grandmothers and even some of their mothers could only dream of. With Angela Merkel as the German Chancellor, Christine Lagarde as head of the International Monetary Fund (IMF), Federica Mogherini as the second woman to head one of the EU's key agencies, the European External Action Service (EEAS), and 60% of university graduates now being female, Europe could be considered a great region in the world for a woman to pursue a career.

Yet, gender equality in Europe is still unfinished business. A 2016 World Economic Forum report noted that, at the current pace, it would take until 2062 for Western Europe to close its economic gender gap. The 2015 Gender Equality Index of the European Institute for Gender Equality (EIGE) states that it could still take more than 100 years for European women to have equal access to the job market and the right to equal pay for equal work. And the "family pictures" of European heads of state after a European Union summit in Brussels, or board sessions of European companies, continue to be dominated by the grey colours of men in suits. All these facts and more demonstrate the lack of gender equality in Europe's decision-making circles.

It has been repeatedly demonstrated that an equal balance of women and men in leadership roles at executive level increases performance both in the public and the private sectors (Harvard Business School, World Economic Forum, Oxford University, Mercer, Catalyst, etc). It seems, however, that awareness of the case for gender diversity has not fully reached Brussels – and the will to address this situation is varied. Many experts argue that increasing the number of women in leadership positions is not only a moral imperative, but is also a requisite for high organisational and team performance. For example, global consultancy firm McKinsey has extensively made the business case for gender diversity in multiple studies and statistics over recent years. In some of these studies, clear correlations were found between a company's performance and the proportion of women serving on the executive board: more women translated to less debt and faster rebound in a crisis. These studies also found that certain leadership styles and behaviours frequently adopted by women are critical to navigating today's complex world ("Women Matter" studies). Similarly, a 2016 Credit Suisse report on European diversity levels found that companies with more women in the boardroom bring better returns and outperform on the stock market.

Gender diversity in leadership means more diverse perspectives, new ways of approaching societies, and an opportunity to diminish obsolete authoritarian models (World Economic Forum 2016). Similarly, in its 2014 Worldwide Women Public Sector Leaders Index, Ernst & Young argues that gender diversity in leadership (and in the workforce) improves innovation, provides creative problem solving, and the capacity to adapt to volatile contexts: "Governments that have a diverse group of people will surely find themselves at an advantage. Making workforces more diverse not only fosters innovation but also helps to drive up quality within that workforce, increasing the pool of talent available and offering a plurality of skills to meet changing needs."

In Brussels, particularly within European institutions, there is growing awareness of these arguments amongst decision-makers, human resources professionals and sections of the public, especially the younger generations. However, effectively addressing the diversity gap remains a challenge within all sectors. Because of the international character of the city and the multiple spheres of influence and power, the case for gender equality and women's professional advancement is being addressed differently – if at all – in the various professional sectors featured in this book. Size, purpose, exclusivity, institutional autonomy, and the fragmentation of women's groups have hindered them from having a more pronounced impact. Cross-fertilisation, sharing of information and good practice, as well as guidance to assist the implementation of different approaches to reach gender equality within and between these circles of women has only just begun!

The business sector is leading the trend, sharing guidelines and good practice in multiple ways and numerous forums in Brussels. Their reform processes are often led by an internal powerful critical mass or by a visionary chief executive officer (CEO). Sometimes their guidelines and policies are simply steered by the strategic objective of improving their reputation or increasing sales among their female customer base. Aware that women are key for their business (according to a Bloomberg feature "women make up 85% of consumer purchases", 2016), many companies and industries understand they need to adapt strategies and bring women onto their management teams. For example, Procter & Gamble's (P&G) acclaimed campaign #WeSeeEqual and viral gender-awareness videos such as "Like A Girl", "We believe in Her" and "P&G Believes in Me" have successfully put the company on the radar screen of women consumers. BNP Paribas Fortis, Cargill, Euroclear, Deloitte, Credit Suisse, British EDF Energy have similar initiatives – not to mention Ernst & Young, McKinsey, Gallup, etc. However, paying attention to gender diversity does not mean there is always consistency in internal implementation.

In Brussels decision-making in key areas – law, security, finance, energy – is still driven by men

In comparison, other sectors – such as policy, public administration, civil society, media, foundations, etc. – in Europe are reacting more slowly. In Brussels decision-making in key areas – law, security, finance, energy – is still driven by men. Brussels conference panels on policy topics tend to be predominantly occupied by male speakers. European member states continue to send larger numbers of male diplomats than female to their representations in Brussels as well as appointing more men to leadership positions in the EU institutions and international bodies. These trends highlight the fact that changes in the European institutions are greatly dependent on EU member state actions.

In the public administration realm, it is the European Commission (EC) that leads the gender diversity track. An awareness trend can be perceived when we observe a Director General of the European Commission deciding that his team members should no longer speak on all male panels (Robert Madelin, Director General in DG Connect, 2010-2015), or First Vice President Frans Timmermans (2014-) and European Commissioner Neven Mimica (2014-) declaring themselves "feminists". More tangible has been the work of former EC Vice President Kristalina Georgieva (from 2014 to 2016), who was responsible for implementing the decision of European Commission President Junker to ensure the appointment of women to 40% of senior EU positions by 2019. That decision is currently filtering down to the dozens of Commission directorates and departments, though not without barriers being put up – the usual resistance to any change, as well as patriarchical resistance from those who fear their promotion opportunities are being reduced. The success of this process remains to be seen.

In addition, the European Commission regularly develops European guidelines relating to women's rights, the pay gap, economic independence, and access to decision-making positions, thereby creating awareness and offering higher standards for European society as a whole. The European Commission is, of course, "just" responsible for proposing legislation, implementing decisions, upholding the EU treaties and managing the day-to-day business of the EU. It cannot oblige EU member states to adopt gender diversity directives. However, with its own 40% gender diversity target and concrete internal changes, the Commission is slowly taking on something of the character of a role model being monitored by advocacy groups and the media.

But despite the good intentions and the fact that equal rights for men and women were one of the EU's founding values in the 1957 Treaty of Rome, these values still don't match the reality, as we will show in detail in the next chapter.

Gender Equality in Europe? – Bringing European Statistics to Life

The latest figures on women and men in decision-making show that the EU is taking a slow but steady path towards gender-balanced representation. This chapter offers some observations and a more detailed picture of gender diversity in the sectors featured elsewhere in this book – the private sector, politics, public administration, media, non-governmental organisations and foundations. We focus mostly on gender balance at the senior level, but also address some instruments and initiatives aimed at improving the gender balance overall.

Private Sector

In the private sector, the evolution towards having more women in decision-making positions is mixed, with some segments advancing faster than others. The number of women in boardrooms has been increasing since 2010, right at the time when the European Commission also made this a priority on its agenda. According to the latest EIGE data in 2017, the proportion of women on the boards of the largest listed companies in the EU doubled from 11.9% in 2010 to 23.9% in 2016. Interestingly, a study carried out by the non-profit organisation European Women on Boards (EWoB, 2016), "Gender Diversity on European Boards. Realising Europe's Potential: Progress and Challenges" found that the trend toward greater gender diversity on boards has been primarily driven by the integration of non-executive or supervisory board female directors as opposed to a progression of women into chair, CEO and executive director positions.

However, men are still making the majority of the decisions at the most senior levels of top management. Only 5.7% of CEO positions are held by women. Overall, there were variations among member states, demonstrating the persistence of different cultural habits and perceptions, as well as variations by industry sector. One of our interviewees, Pastora Valero, who works at multinational technology company CISCO in Brussels, told us that: "there are 23% to 33% women in entry level or junior roles in CISCO, but when you move to more senior roles women represent only 11% of the leadership. And females make up only 5% of CEOs in the IT industry." Other companies such as lobbying and public affairs have a larger share of women – as prominently featured in POLITICO Europe in 2016, where 13 women who were heading such outfits in Brussels were profiled. Shéhérazade Semsar-de Boisséson, one of our interviewees, from the business side of POLITICO Europe, attributes this tendency partly to women's communication skills. On the other hand, the legal sector presents a very different image. As Salomé Cisnal de Ugarte, a lawyer and one of our other interviewees, put it "… women are definitely under represented. For instance, in Brussels, the legal market, there are very few women partners. The associate level, it's probably equal, but then when it gets to partnership it gets definitely less."

The absence of women in executive positions in the private sector is further accentuated by the pay gap as revealed in the European Commission 2017 report on equality between women and men in the EU. Numerous companies have developed professional development opportunities for women, mentoring programmes and codes of conduct to address diversity, but successes and general changes have been infrequent at best.

Politics

Despite some progress made over the last decades, women's participation in politics remains a challenge. Women account for less than a third of the members of national parliaments in the EU. This figure varies considerably across the member states, from 46.1% in Sweden to 9.5% in Hungary, according to the EIGE's latest data on women and men in decision-making positions. The picture in the European Parliament tells a similar story. Danuta Hübner, a Member of the European Parliament and one of our interviewees cited the following statistic: "As of now, in 2016 at 36.9%, the percentage of women in the European Parliament is very slightly higher than in the previous legislature (35.8%). This increase may not look imposing, but it is the national political context that determines the outcomes." Out of the 15 presidents that the European Parliament has elected since its inception, only two have been women: Simone Veil (1979-1982) and Nicole Fontaine (1999-2002). Once elected, another challenge is for these women to get prominent places in the organigram – such as Vice President, committee chairs or delegation leaders.

Women are still under-represented in political decision-making, particularly at the highest levels, across Europe. As Margot Wallström, Foreign Minister of Sweden, said during our interview with her: "Among the 28 foreign ministers of the member states we are only three women. I think that's bad. Strikingly few still." A closer look shows that the gender imbalance is further reflected in who gets what kind of ministerial position. Women politicians often end up with the "softer" portfolios such as family affairs, education, health and culture. Men tend to get assigned to more "hard" subject matters such as economics, technology and defence. All this continues to reinforce traditional stereotypes about women's and men's roles and expertise.

> *Women politicians often end up with the "softer" portfolios such as family affairs, education, health and culture*

Becoming head of state and government is an even more challenging path for a woman: in the EU's 28 countries, only 17% of the country's leaders were women in 2016 (European Parliament Briefing, 2016). In local government – where decisions impact directly on the daily lives of men and women – 2017 figures collected by the European Commission show that 85% of mayoral positions in the EU-28 are held by men, while 65% of the membership of municipal councils (or their equivalent) is male.

In 2016, however, we witnessed a wave of female politicians running for mayor of major European cities, such as Rome, Barcelona, and Paris (see: The Guardian's article "Can cities be feminist? Inside the global rise of female mayors", October 10, 2016 or iNews' "Meet the new female mayors of Europe's major cities", 20.06.2016). Many of these women represent new or smaller parties, bringing new faces to the local government level, which has so far been dominated by men. Some of them have set different priorities in their administrations, such as tackling environmental issues, public transportation shortages, corruption, or housing policy issues.

> *Gender quotas are a must. Politics are full of quotas anyway – geographical, political affiliation, age*

Yet, as a joint Women in Parliament (WIP; since February 2017 renamed Women Political Leaders Global Forum) and World Bank report in 2015 concluded, the glass ceiling in politics remains iron-clad; party politics, campaign financing and sexism in politics and media continue to be major barriers to women running for political office. For transformational change in politics, "Gender quotas are a must. Politics are full of quotas anyway –

geographical, political affiliation, age etc." says Silvana Koch Mehrin, former Member of the European Parliament and founder of Women Political Leaders Global Forum. Other initiatives to encourage women to run for office, such as "Women for Election" in Ireland, are only slowly taking off.

Public Administration

The administrative pillar of the European Parliament has also been dealing with diversity challenges. According to the Women in the European Parliament Report from March 2017, out of 50 Director General and Director level positions, 17 are held by women, or 16.7% and 29.8% respectively. Over time the placement of women in senior management positions has actually varied greatly over the years, from 33.3% in 2008 to 36.4% in 2012, 0% in 2013 and 11.1% in 2016. Nevertheless, women consistently make up more than 80% of administrative and support staff. While the language of the European Parliament boasts a commitment to gender balance and women's professional development, our observations are different. The internal dynamics of this highly political institution are such that the politics of political parties and the member states' representations as well as cultural and political differences stand in the way of allowing any coordinated efforts to make the European Parliament an institution where women feel supported and have clear prospects for professional advancement. There have not been any noteworthy attempts to create women's alliances across parties nor to systematically promote gender diversity at the top of the administration. As Francesca Ratti (the recently retired Deputy Secretary General of the European Parliament) observes: "Gender diversity is unfortunately not considered as a prestigious or powerful subject to fight for. Not only men but also many political women do not go beyond repetitive declarations nor support a sustained engagement in the battle for gender diversity and equal opportunities, eventually for fear of being condemned into a women ghetto and excluded from other 'more political' issues."

Not only men but also many political women do not go beyond repetitive declarations

The European Commission's administrative workforce is composed of 54.9% of women, but these women represent only 27.5% of the Commission's senior and middle management. The figures vary for the other EU key institutions and services. For example, the General Secretariat of the Council of the

European Union organigram shows a massive proportion of men in the top and middle management positions. Christine Roger, who became Director General responsible for Justice and Home Affairs in July 2015, is the only woman in the Council on this level.

In its 2014 Worldwide Index of Women as Public Sector Leaders, Ernst & Young showed that women represent less than 20% of public sector leadership across the G20. The study showed that only one European country – the United Kingdom – has one-third or more women in leadership roles across the public sector. Among the 20 top-ranking positions, there were only four European countries and the European Commission. One of them, France is considered as a case where quotas (introduced in 2012) had a direct impact on the number of women in senior posts. On the other hand, in Germany, while the federal government introduced a 30% quota for women on the boards of DAX-listed companies in November 2013, so far there has not been an equivalent quota for the civil service.

Another noteworthy practice at the local level is the gender budgeting developed in one of the Brussels municipalities, Ixelles. Here, local politician Viviane Teitelbaum (Alderwoman in charge of Finance at Ixelles Municipality and Member of the Brussels Region Parliament) has successfully pioneered the application of gender mainstreaming into the municipality's budgetary process. Gender responsive budgeting (GRB) is an internationally recognised tool that ensures the achievement of de facto gender equality and contributes to the effective allocation of public funds. In practice, this means a gender-based assessment of budgets, incorporating a gender perspective at all levels of the budgetary process and restructuring revenues and expenditures in order to promote gender equality. "This experience could pave the way for multiple applications, at the local, regional, national and European levels", says Claudia De Decker Ritter, Director of Cleverland, Senior Associate at Management Centre Europe and President of the Sofia Foundation.

Media, Civil Society & Foundations

Data on gender in Brussels' other key sectors such as media, foundations, and non-governmental organisations are difficult to come by.

The city hosts one of the world's largest press corps, with numerous national media outlets having correspondents, and even more freelance journalists.

The Association of Professional Journalists reports 602 male (63.9%) and 337 female (36.1%) accredited journalists (October 2016). While women outnumber men in university-level and practice-based journalism programmes and there are increasing numbers of women in media, the organisational culture of media remains largely masculine and women are still significantly under-represented at the decision-making level such as editors or heads of section, according to data collected by EIGE and published in its "Women and Media Report" in 2015. On average women represent 40% of journalists in Brussels-based international media, but hold only 3% of the decision-making posts. This imbalance not only inhibits women's efforts to develop their careers, but the absence of women at decision-making levels influences media content and what is conveyed as news.

When it comes to the non-profit sector and non-governmental organisations working with the EU institutions, gender-related data is very scattered. Most surveys and research about gender diversity by leading companies such as Ernst & Young, Mercer, etc. have largely neglected this sector. There are mostly only perceptions, anecdotal evidence and fragments of data, as Joanna Maycock, Secretary General of the European Women's Lobby, confirmed.

Brussels civil society is not a monolithic entity – it includes membership associations, advocacy groups, non-governmental organisations and public policy or research institutions covering diverse policy subjects and pursuing different goals. As Claudia Ritter, co-founder/president of the Sofia Foundation and a certified executive and leadership coach has observed, while women who came to Brussels in the late 1980s and early 1990s could assume the functions of office directors of regional representations and social NGOs, they witnessed how men gradually moved into senior management positions as their organisations became more powerful. As Claudia says: "The glass ceiling is alive and well in the non-profit sector, even if there are significant differences in mind-set and approach, between cultures and generations." In Brussels, while the overwhelming majority of non-profit employees are women, opportunities to advance are limited. A mapping exercise led by the German Marshall Fund of the United States in 2013, assessing 13 think tanks with offices in Brussels, showed that only 2 were headed by women.

> *women witnessed how men gradually moved into senior management positions as their organisations became more powerful*

Moreover, many events and panels organised by the top think tanks are still disproportionally dominated by male speakers, as research by the Brussels-based initiative EU Panel Watch shows (Monitoring Month 2016 "Who's dominating EU debates", "Where are the women in EU debates?").

Finally, the philanthropy sector continues to be among the most conservative sectors. While their umbrella organisation, the European Foundation Centre (EFC) which represents approximately 200 foundations, up to 2017 had a female chair of its management committee, which now has 3 women and 4 men, on the national level most foundations remain the realm of "old boys". Foundations headed by women such as the Gulbenkian Foundation in Lisbon, the Barrow Cadbury Trust or the European Cultural Foundation are still rare.

A first step towards breaking old habits by bringing in gender mainstreaming as a tool to the work of some foundations was an initiative of the EFC's Gender Equality Network – composed of the King Baudouin Foundation, the Barrow Cadbury Trust, the OAK Foundation, Mama Cash, Sabanci Foundation and the Joseph Rowntree Charitable Trust. It developed some guidelines to facilitate a better understanding of gender, and promotes the use of a "gender lens" throughout the foundations' work, including gender responsive budgeting. Their first report (2015) entitled "Grant-making with a gender lens", looked at a number of foundation programmes, showing how including a gender lens leads to more equitable, impactful and sustainable outcomes. But as Françoise Pissart, Director at the King Baudoin Foundation, states in her interview, bringing a gender lens into the structures and work of foundations is not at all automatic. Cultural differences, for example, make it difficult to develop a common agenda. Anglo-Saxon foundations are much more willing to look at staff composition while foundations from Southern Europe or certain sectors such as banking display more reluctance to adopt gender-sensitive approaches. As Francoise says: "If you want to change something at the European level you have to be patient and go step by step."

Overall, it can be said that women are more likely to hold mid-level leadership positions within EU non-profit organisations and they remain under-represented in top governing positions. This has also been confirmed by research done by Claus, Callahan & Sandlin ("Culture and Leadership: Women in Non-Profit and For-Profit Leadership Positions within the European Union", 2013) who examined women's leadership positions within non-profit and for-profit organisations in 51 companies in the European Union.

Why is Change so Slow in Europe?

With all the awareness and discussions on diversity and the need for more women in leadership positions in the European (policy) context, why do gender-based barriers remain so persistent in today's Europe/world and why is parity of opportunities and rights taking so long to become a reality?

The answer is both simple and complex.

It is simple in the sense that most of the surveys carried out by well-respected universities and research institutions point in a similar direction: patriarchical traditions and norms, conscious and unconscious bias, as well as stereotyping of women and men tell us what masculinity and femininity mean. This is reproduced through education systems (formal and familial), social interaction and amplified by the media. This all contributes to reinforcing the tendency for power to remain elite male territory. Indeed, most of the time, it is enough to say the word "leader" and the majority of people will visualise a man.

But the answer is also complex precisely because these stereotypes are so deeply entrenched in us, in our psyches, in our communities and broader society, consciously and often unconsciously. In fact, stereotypes are powerful not only because they are the result of many centuries of patterns of survival and socialisation, but also because they are part of how the human brain functions. Modern psychology and neuroscience show that stereotypes serve to cluster people into simplified groups with a variety of expected traits (transmitted from previous generations and through socialisation repetitions). These then help us to navigate the world without being overwhelmed by information (Journal of Cognitive Neuroscience, 2016).

But this "brain simplification program" comes at a high price: women are still unfairly treated in the workplace, in their career progression and in general, in great part because of bias and stereotypes. While we do not necessarily perceive women as "victims", we cannot be blind to the – sometimes blatant, sometimes subtle, many times unintentional – discrimination that many women still face in the 21st century.

The path to leadership is disproportionately hard and stressful for women: women are still expected to carry out most family duties; women are paid 16% less than men for equal work in Europe; and 75% of professional women in Europe, including in top management, have experienced some form of sexual harassment during their careers and suffer from the impunity that often protects perpetrators (European Commission, European Union Fundamental Rights Agency, Sorbonne University, McKinsey, and others).

The path to leadership is disproportionately hard and stressful for women

Thus changing mentalities and perceptions, behaviours and action is fundamental to changing societies. All this is vital for women (and other under- and unrepresented groups) to enjoy fair and equal treatment, and contribute their share of talent to the sectors where they work.

Transforming our societies is a process that requires long-term vision, a strategy, and sustained investment in (re)education and in (re)designing organisations in ways that reduce the space for bias. It requires constant vigilance, determination, commitment and indeed leadership, as we will explore later in the book. Despite the efforts made over recent decades to increase awareness about gender stereotypes and their negative consequences in women's (and men's) lives, the actual transformation process (of mentalities and societies) is lengthy and remains challenging.

Despite these obstacles, there is new and evolving research confirming that it is possible to achieve gender equality. The first piece of good news is that recent research has shown that it is possible to unlearn discriminatory beliefs and attitudes, and to teach our modern brains to question the old traditional models and dogmas that have structured our identities and roles in the past (e.g. The Oxford Handbook of Human Development and Culture, 2015). The second piece of good news is that there are multiple organisations and individuals working towards these changes. Now it is about finding ways to create more synergies and opportunities for learning good practices and amplifying the messages that need to be heard.

And, finally, there are in Europe today some role models who show it is possible for women to challenge and overcome traditional roles, women who – in spite of all the barriers – became leaders. These women are paving the way for the success of other women, even when they do not proactively engage in gender-related advocacy – like Angela Merkel or Federica Mogherini. These women are powerful women role models. Just by being there they challenge patriarchical structures and mentalities. These women, and many others, show it is possible for a woman to lead, and to lead successfully; to stand their ground, handle tough negotiations, make hard decisions and command a complex structure. But most women role models are not as visible as them and much more remains to be done to shed light on the richness and diversity of women's leadership, in Europe and globally.

Just by being there they challenge patriarchical structures and mentalities

This takes us back to the raison d'être of this book and to the content of Part II: the stories of 14 women leaders in Brussels. These diverse women – with distinct profiles, backgrounds and leadership styles – are contributing to making Europe more diverse and "colourful". These are some of the women showing that there are many different ways in which a woman can lead. We believe this diversity of voices, styles and views is particularly critical in the historical moment we are currently living through, when Europe and its existence as a project for collaboration is under stress. This European project, born out of the resolution of its Founding Fathers, a group of male leaders with a powerful vision, needs a revision and modernisation – and diversity needs to be at its core.

The Europe we want is a Europe where human rights and equality are not only nice concepts, but facts. A Europe where "no woman will get a job simply because of her gender, but no woman will be denied a job because of her gender either", to quote the words of former European Commissioner Viviane Reding. And a Europe whose joint decisions, structures and "family picture" accurately reflects the gender diversity – and the diversity at large – of European citizens, their aspirations and their talents.

PART II

PORTRAITS OF WOMEN LEADING THE WAY

Salomé Cisnal de Ugarte

Belgian/Spanish. Partner at an international law firm.
Striving for excellence, familiar with leadership. Lawyer in
antitrust and EU competition law.

Concentrate on what is Essential

A Basque Mother – and the Product of Different Influences

Salomé is an exceptional and widely known lawyer, educated in Spain, the
US and Italy. She identifies key people and access to education as decisive
factors in her life which brought her to where she is today. Being accepted
to Harvard Law School in her early 20s opened a whole new world to her:
"It gave me the possibility of getting the best legal education, and it gave
me access to a network, to a group of people that were just exceptional on
all accounts."

Salomé's mother, from the Basque region of Spain, played an instrumental role in her development. While Spanish society was patriarchal, Basque women continued to pass down through the generations the conviction that women are powerful, strong and independent. Salomé describes her mother as the quintessential example of this strong Basque matriarchal mentality, intelligent, determined, and very conscious of the role of women in the 20th century. Salomé's mother was not able to pursue an international career herself given the nature of society during the dictatorship of Francisco Franco (1936-1975). It was only in the later years of Franco's rule, known as the "Spanish miracle" (1959-1974), when Salomé was born, that Spain saw some economic and political liberalisation and the country began to catch up economically with its European neighbours. Democracy emerged in 1982, and in 1986 Spain joined the European Community.

Salomé's mother had a clear vision for her daughter's development and professional accomplishments: "She set a task for me: to become what I am today. She encouraged me to get here. She made sure that I received the best education I could get, she sent me and my brother to a German-speaking school, and to the best universities in Spain and the US to study law. She was an inspiration to get the best out of us!" Her mother also taught her that creating a family was as important as having a professional career. These days, Salomé is with her husband successfully raising their four children and pursuing a fulfilling career, just as her mother wished. For this to be possible, Salomé has had to focus on what is essential, to plan and to delegate the tasks that are not a priority. "My mom also taught me to be aware of my limits, so I have never had a problem about hiring household help, a babysitter or a nanny". And Salomé adds that having a spouse as a true partner at home also helps.

Many other people have helped Salomé along the way, personally and professionally. As Salomé puts it: "I was lucky to have many people around me who helped me in different

You need to have the courage to sometimes go and ask for help

ways. You need to have the courage to sometimes go and ask for help. Then you get the insights of people who have already made it, or people who are at a different stage of their career."

Not only Gender Discrimination

As Salomé was building her professional career in 1990s Brussels, she experienced prejudice and barriers. Not only because she was a woman, but also because she was a young woman, a mother and from the south of Europe: "My first firm was mostly staffed by German men who were practically groomed for partnership". It was her assertiveness that got Salomé her first job as a young mother. When interviewing for that job, she was asked by the male interviewer how she was planning to combine work and a child. Arguing she was no less capable because of being a mother, she raised a counter question: "Do you have children?" When her interviewer responded with "Yes", Salomé replied: "Well, I am willing to do it exactly as you do. I will try to combine my personal skills, my intelligence and being a professional during the day and in the evening take care of my children, like all daddies do."

Salomé felt privileged to work for a big German law firm, but she was particularly happy to work in their Brussels office. At that time (1990s), working mothers were still very much frowned upon; there were very few women lawyers working in that firm and none of them had children. So she took an important lesson from this first experience: "They ultimately hired me. That taught me that you have to be assertive, otherwise you will never get the opportunity."

No Secret Formula

Combining work and family means organising well. Salomé admits that there is a lot of planning, setting priorities, employing help, etc. She and her husband work as a team managing two careers and the family. Salomé tried to approach her life as a project: "In the beginning perhaps you see your professional career, you see it as a plan… But then you realise that it is not like that, especially if you want children." With time, she came to realise that her main goal was to be able to maintain a professional career while having a personal life and a family. That meant being able to balance both sides: "I left some time in between children, to be able to go back to work. I have seen that in law firms, women come back, then get pregnant immediately, then leave, come back, leave again. And after the third child, they have lost their jobs. I am not saying this is right, but since I have seen it, I took measures and planned. That is the cruel reality. Every child also needs attention, so ultimately, you need to give that to them too."

Salomé is convinced that women can have it all, but ultimately "All" is about what it means to each person. And while a woman can have everything, she needs to be aware of the implications: "Nothing is for free, everything has an impact and a consequence. You can have it all but not all at the same time. There is a time for everything." The best way to ensure that you end up "having it all" is adaptability: "You have a plan, an idea, a project, but you have to adapt to the situation, to the timing, to your wishes, your needs, and your own limitations." For her, having been able to sustain a professional life – which includes not only her job, but also her leadership roles as a board member of the Harvard University Club Belgium, the Harvard Alumni Association (HAA) and the American Chamber of Commerce to the European Union (AmChamEU) – alongside a personal life is her biggest accomplishment. Salomé's personal formula for achievement includes her capacity to prioritise and adapt to circumstances; her determination and self-esteem, and self-awareness of her abilities and limitations. And it was also about being herself, not pretending she was a man.

You can have it all but not all at the same time. There is a time for everything

Leadership as a Skill or an Art?

Salomé's time at Harvard allowed for early exposure to the matter of leadership. According to her, leadership "is an art that motivates, guides and empowers other people to achieve a mutually agreed goal, a mission or an objective." But for her, talent and skills are not enough to be a leader: "You can have the skills to be a fantastic leader, but if you never get the position, or the ability to exercise those skills, you're unable to become a real leader." This is one of the factors that make it difficult for women to go beyond the glass ceiling and become influential. In law firms, according to Salomé, leadership is not just measured by how many people you manage. It is measured in terms of how you reach your objectives; how you are able to motivate and empower the team to get the desired result. As Salomé says: "I have also worked in a company as in-house counsel for some years and there, leadership was very much promoted and furthered. It was very interesting because it allowed me to see leadership as it is seen in business … in terms of how many people you have below you, how many people you are managing, and it is all structured around that." Leadership with values is also an integral part of how Salomé operates based on her Harvard education, as she recognises. Beyond the traditional definitions of leadership as authority and power, she stresses respect, honesty, integrity and accountability as relevant. She acknowledges that leadership styles have evolved enormously because professional life nowadays is different from what it was 20 years ago, and as a result of having more women in the public eye.

For Salomé, "women are typically known to be more inclusive, more cooperative, with a different kind of leadership. Men are more directive and transactional." Having said this, she feels ambivalent about the standardisation of men's versus women's leadership styles. For her, it is more about people and less about generalisations: "I think it depends on people. I have met very good leaders who are men and who are as cooperative as the best women in the world, and I have also met women who are not."

Salomé's own leadership style is consistent with her definition of leadership with values. She explains that she always tries to excel and expects that from others; she empowers, gives structure, organisation, a sense of direction and motivation to her team while avoiding micro-management: "While I try to motivate others, I also try to be inclusive in the sense of creating a team and knowing we are there to achieve a certain goal. Being inclusive doesn't mean that you don't get to any decision or result. You still have to drive the group and get a result. I am very results-driven."

Brussels: a City that Brings the Best of Many Worlds

Salomé loves Brussels. While she never thought she would "end up" here, she now sees it as a place that offers the best of many worlds. "It is self-selection: the people you find in Brussels are fantastic. It is always easier to stay at home (in your own country), close to your family and old friends. Here, you have to start from scratch. Here, people have left their comfort zone to come to Brussels, to work for Europe. These people are usually exceptional and extremely interesting." Salomé is also very aware of the Belgian hosts and their different cultures. Language skills, interests in different cultures, and the ability to move from one "bubble" to another and adapt are part of a particular skill set for people moving here: "If you want to move between these different worlds, you have to speak languages. I speak five languages and I use them constantly and that's wonderful because you can move from one culture to another. You must also be able to understand Belgian culture, to understand Belgian politics and EU politics, and be able to move from one to the other and adapt. That's what makes Brussels special."

Thanks to the presence of the European institutions and an increasing awareness of the gender gap, the situation for women has greatly improved in terms of flexibility to accommodate parenting and a professional life, but certain sectors such as private law firms are slow to catch up, says Salomé. Brussels is a good place to work as it offers conditions that make it easier for working women, such as home support, child-care and a school system that provides after-school activities, as well as tax deductions for child-care. Moreover, the city also possesses a lot of networks and networking opportunities that offer professional help and provide access to new career opportunities as well as information. As Salomé says, these are networks that need to be built and nurtured by men and women alike: "Networks are essential in Brussels. They take time to build up – you are not just meeting somebody, you have an opportunity to nurture that relationship." For Salomé, influence derives from the right combination of contacts and people's capacity and knowledge.

Developing a Woman's Legal Career in Brussels

Salomé's former law firm Crowell & Moring, where she worked until June 2017, is currently headed by a woman (in the US) and the board is composed of 50% women. However, this has not yet led to the same balance among partners. Salomé still sees many women drop out at associate level, becoming in-house legal counsel in private companies, or moving to the European institutions. In general, the legal sector in Brussels continues to be very unbalanced regarding gender representation at the senior level, but Salomé believes that "there is recognition and a desire to change and to give women access to leading positions and management positions." While the sector is slow to catch up, there are initiatives to advance the situation: there are networks such as the Women's Competition Network, which brings together women lawyers for peer counselling and mentoring. Salomé's former law firm organises regular get-togethers for female employees.

Aside from the support structures for women, there are attempts to involve men in raising awareness, though this remains a difficult task. Men engage with gender equality when it suits them: for example, they attend events with external speakers, such as in-house counsels of client firms, and although Salomé notes that they probably do this for career reasons, she sees this as at least a start. The key point Salomé wants to get across to men is that it is not just about including women for the benefit of women, it is about ensuring that everyone – including men – benefits from a more complete picture that takes different perspectives into consideration. In Salomé's view, men need to be constantly reminded that women are their peers, that they are just as good leaders as the men are: "It's just making sure that women are always there – they are part of the equation!"

Salomé has come to regard quotas for women's employment as beneficial. She sees them as a way of raising awareness, changing attitudes, and creating the infrastructure and environment to open up the jobs market. "I thought quotas weren't necessary when I was young and naïve", she says. But now she believes that positive measures will give women more access to decision-making positions and that this will lead to a change in mentalities:

I thought quotas weren't necessary when I was young and naïve

"The picture of a board meeting ten years ago was all white men but nowadays you have some degree of racial diversity there, some women. So things are changing, but are they changing fast enough?" She argues that to change the current situation, concrete measures and infrastructure are essential. That means measures that include organisational and work environment flexibility (e.g. remote work, work based on results and not hours spent in the office, etc). She passionately concludes that society needs to understand that the lack of diversity is a problem, and that it means a lot of talent is being lost: "It can't be that we send our daughters to university, they start a job and then drop out because they are made to believe that having a family and a professional career is not compatible. That is a huge waste for them and for society. It needs to change!"

Wisdom, Tips, Dos & Don'ts for a Leader-to-be

Make **goals** and a plan to **achieve** them. And then be ready to **adjust** the plan.

Look for opportunities to **help other women**!

Don't be afraid to **ask for help** – up, down, sideways.

Don't try to be and **act like a man**.

You can **lead** and also have a **full family life**.

Build and use **networks** in your sphere and beyond.

Ana Gomes

Portuguese. Member of the European Parliament since 2004. Born under the Portuguese dictatorship, Ana is known for asking the uncomfortable questions that others do not dare to ask.

Be Yourself!

A Rebel since Early Days

Ana is a fighter and her volcanic energy is known to all those around her. She is determined, believes in what she does and rarely gives up on her objectives. In Brussels, she is known as a champion of human rights and democracy. In her country of origin, Portugal, and elsewhere, she is known as a woman who never fears to speak up and voice her opinions.

When discussing the experiences that brought Ana to where she is today, she identifies three key periods.

The first of these was living under the dictatorship in Portugal of António de Oliveira Salazar, who wielded power for more than 30 years (1933-1968), a regime inspired by conservative, nationalist and religious beliefs and ideologies. To ensure their survival, the dictatorship resorted to authoritarian and repressive measures, with strict state censorship in place. At that time, Ana was a young teenager curious about what was happening around her. However, her mother forbade Ana to ask her questions about the evolving situation in the country: "Out of fear that I would also raise these kinds of questions outside the family. Being forbidden just motivated me to be even more inquisitive about the nature of the regime. Why shouldn't I speak? Why shouldn't I ask questions about the regime? That was what led me into politics." Ana was 14 years old when the dictator Salazar fell ill and was removed from office. She had just turned 20 when in 1974, the Carnation Revolution took place in Lisbon and a military coup, organised by left-wing Portuguese military officers, overthrew the nationalist regime, to the joy of a Portuguese population tired of repression and fear.

The second defining period came after Ana had graduated from university in 1979. She sat the exams to enter the Ministry of Foreign Affairs: "I always enjoyed speaking languages and following international affairs. I found out that this career had been forbidden to women until 1975, so that motivated me to follow that path. I suddenly switched from being a lawyer to being a diplomat, with the additional challenge of representing a new democratic Portugal and helping to build it."

I was flooded with letters from girls from all over Portugal … If I could do it, so could others

The third period came when she became the first Ambassador of Portugal to Indonesia, actively contributing to the process leading to the independence of East Timor, and the establishment of diplomatic relations between Portugal and Indonesia, after 24 years of political tensions. As Ambassador, Ana became highly visible back in Portugal and this helped to change her perception of her own mission: "It gave me a lot of exposure in our media, and showed me I had an obligation to become a role model for younger women who wanted to move into the diplomatic service and public service. … I was flooded with letters from girls from all over Portugal who found it fascinating that there was a woman in such a tough position. … It was risky and difficult, and yet I was a young woman doing it. If I could do it, so could others." In 2003, Ana joined the leadership of the Socialist party and again switched careers: "I am in politics and I am happy."

The Inspiration of Others

Encouraged by her mother, Ana read the story of Marie Curie at an early age. According to Ana, this woman scientist working for humanity in a traditionally masculine area, going through tremendous adversity, gave her the sense that anything was possible and that she, equally, could do anything she wanted.

Living in a very reactionary environment during the dictatorship in Portugal was difficult. Ana says: "You can either be very depressed, or decide to go and fight it. I was always in the latter mood: continually reminding myself that as an individual, as a woman, I am able to do anything." Despite the general context of political repression and fear, Ana's family, teachers and friends instilled in her the sense that she could achieve whatever she wanted. As a teenager, Ana had joined a clandestine youth organisation, which fought against the authoritarian Salazar regime. Those group dynamics motivated and sustained her political development. Ana describes herself as always having been a team person; she is convinced that individuals cannot achieve important objectives alone. They need to work in groups, build alliances and support systems. Throughout her life, and especially also later when she became a mother, her family and her former husband's family consistently supported her: "That gave me the space, the peace of mind, to be able to invest in my own personal realisation." Ana explains that she does not separate professional from personal fulfilment. Today a delighted grandmother, she says that both aspects are fundamental to her: "I would have been very unhappy if I had only succeeded in one of these dimensions."

Subtle and Blatant Gender Discrimination

Having found her years as an activist in the underground student movement empowering, Ana's experience of gender discrimination first started when she entered a professional career as a diplomat at the Portuguese Foreign Ministry. Ana received discriminatory gender comments throughout her career and regularly witnessed women being victims of discrimination. Whenever possible, Ana challenged such behaviour. However, in 1989, when she served as diplomatic Counsellor at the Portuguese Embassy in Tokyo, Ana accompanied her Ambassador to a meeting with an older Member of the Japanese Parliament. The Ambassador relied on her expertise in the subject matter to lead the meeting and engage with the Japanese counterpart. The situation was far from simple, Ana recalls: "He (the Japanese Member of Parliament) wouldn't look at me. He would only talk to the Ambassador. I really felt for the first time that I was being discriminated against simply because I was a woman. Never had I been in such a humiliating situation." Ana's instinctive strategy was to keep her cool and remain focused on the task at hand, while ensuring that the Japanese Member of Parliament would not realise how upset she was with the situation.

I Lead because I am a Fighter

Today, Ana defines herself as "a political animal that needs to be in society". What works for her to get ahead is to work hard and enjoy what she does. What drives her is the

I lead because I'm a fighter and because I tell the truth

ambition to make changes and to tell the truth, even when others tell lies. She aims to make the difference, see the big picture, and never give up the freedom to speak her mind. With experience, she has become more selective of the causes she invests in. She became aware of her leadership style when people started to knock on her door – drawn by their belief that she would give them a voice. She concludes: "I lead because I'm a fighter and because I tell the truth. That's my way of leading. If my aim was to have power, I would be very frustrated. My aim is to make a difference, to be able to help people understand what is at stake, mobilise them to change things, and help the people that I can help." Used to finding herself in uncomfortable situations where she is contested – sometimes aggressively – because she tells the truth, Ana gradually learnt to make the most of her strengths and alliances.

Knowing Yourself

For Ana, a good leader is someone with the ability to articulate clear objectives and who speaks their mind. On the differences between men's and women's leadership styles, Ana believes most differences come from education and socialisation. Ana believes men are often educated by family and society to be more ambitious, to set higher professional goals and to achieve those at any cost. Women often tend to weigh up costs and benefits, think about how to be even more effective, and give more significance to personal ties. Women are also better at using their emotional intelligence, i.e. they are more self-aware, empathetic, good in interpersonal and social skills, and emphasise collaborative and team work.

Absence of Leadership in Brussels Today

Ana considers that the city's power dynamics require a solid and proactive political strategy and good communication skills from leaders. A long-term defender of women's rights, Ana decided to bring a gender lens into her political leadership work: "I didn't want to be confined to a niche. I wanted to fight for women's rights and human rights, especially in the areas of security and defence policy and practice." As a Member of the European Parliament, Ana has been trying to bring a human rights approach to policy-making on internal security, the fight against terrorism, and the management of migration and refugees. Ana believes it is extremely important to understand the role of the media in Europe, especially today, in the process of framing and changing societies and mentalities. In this context, Ana recommends women become more familiar and confident with working with the media, including through training in how to use media and communication tools. She considers the role of female journalists, commentators, bloggers and other social media actors to be crucial in helping to bring about change in society.

Women – and Men's – Pressure and Assertiveness are Crucial to Advancing Gender Parity in Brussels

Ana recalls her collaboration with the European Women's Lobby during the run-up to the European Parliament elections in 2009 and the constitution of the new European Commission, when they demanded a minimum of one third of women in the College of Commissioners in the second Barroso Commission: "I think that, because we were so assertive, they took us seriously. Now it is the new normal!"

In Brussels, women have both challenges and opportunities, and the relation between these two is, according to Ana, to a large extent in the hands of women themselves: "If women take themselves seriously and

because we were so assertive, they took us seriously. Now it is the new normal!

tight, they will be seriously recognised", she says. Quotas are an important political development. For Ana, the struggle for gender equality is a process that requires both political will and adequate legislation. She would like to see European parties develop their own "Emily's List", the US Democratic Party initiative that has proactively supported hundreds of women to win elections, at different government levels. To obtain results, it is fundamental to press individual member states and not only the Brussels EU institutions. In this context, Ana is exasperated about Portugal: "In the new (Portuguese) State Council, there is only one woman among 20 members. It is outrageous!" Nonetheless, she remarks that women's critical mass today is much stronger than it was a few years ago – and not just because of the women involved but also because of the men: "It is vital that men understand that gender parity is a crucial question in the quality of society and democracy. Involving young people and educating them about a culture of equality is fundamental." For Ana, it is not simply about having more women in decision-making positions: it is about having rights and developing more balanced gender relationships in the different bodies.

This means that women must be themselves, instead of trying to copy men. They should proactively bring in new perspectives, ideas and tactics; collaborate with each other; challenge the mainstream agendas, and demand more inclusivity and diversity. In this context, Ana refers to her current work as a member of the Justice, Home Affairs, and Civic Liberties (LIBE) Committee of the European Parliament: "The LIBE Committee has an incredible number of women in top positions, and I think that makes the difference. In some points we can reach to each other on a personal level across party lines. It is a bit audacious of me to say so, but I really believe this makes a difference."

Wisdom, Tips, Dos & Don'ts for Women Leaders-to-be

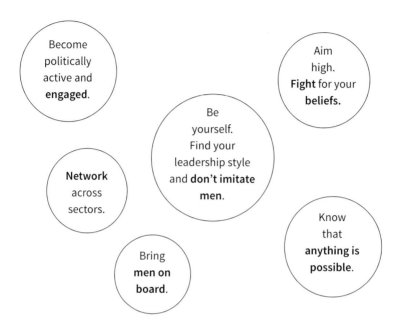

Louise Harvey

British. Chair of Strategic Communication at FTI Consulting Brussels. A woman who defines her own path. Recognised for her accomplishments as a diplomat and as a business-woman.

Be Fearless: Opportunities are there for the Taking

An Unconventional Path

Louise Harvey has spent over 25 years in international consulting. She is a poised woman, displaying maturity and self-confidence. At the age of 18, Louise began her career in the British Foreign Service – an institution that until 1973 required women to leave when they got married. Louise was posted to various countries such as Malaysia, Tanzania and The Netherlands – and was honoured with the award of Member of the Royal Victorian Order (MVO).

Louise's first diplomatic experience at the age of 21 was in Kuala Lumpur. There she found herself among expatriates who clung on to old-fashioned traditions such as women retreating after dinner to leave men discussing politics: "Can you imagine it? It was like Downtown Abbey in 1912."

Back in London, Louise started working on EU affairs in the Foreign & Commonwealth Office (FCO), which led her to switch into the consultancy and public affairs world. Those were the years (early 1990s) when the single European market was being launched, so businesses were struggling to understand what the then-called "European Communities" (EC) were and how they would impact businesses.

Helping understand the "new Europe" rapidly became a flourishing business. Louise was well-placed to enter this emerging market and she did not miss the chance when an opportunity came up to work at a public relations company. Her work took her frequently to Brussels where she eventually settled and co-founded Blueprint Partners; this was subsequently sold to FTI Consulting in 2008, the company she currently chairs. She was the first female president of the British Chamber of Commerce in Belgium and is a current member of the Board of AmCham EU as well as other organisations. Thanks to these and other major accomplishments, Louise was recognised for her services to British business in Belgium, being awarded an OBE (Officer of the Order of the British Empire).

Keep Going!

For Louise, her professional development followed a steady evolution. Looking back, she does not remember any "big bang or anything like that". Instead, it was the way she was brought up and a sequence of experiences that led her to become the high-level professional she is today.

Louise's mother was her prime influence. At a time when so many people around Louise advised her just to get married and learn to serve tea, it was her mother who impressed on Louise the importance of being independent, of striving to have her own income and career. Her mum was there at the moments when Louise had to make important choices and supported her through life. It was Louise's mother, too, who instilled in her a sense of determination to pursue her professional path and have a family: "There have been times over the years when it was quite challenging to be working and be a mother." This imperative to keep going is something Louise wants to pass on to the next generation, notably her own daughter – and more broadly to the young women she frequently mentors: "It is important that young women think about the varied elements when making their career. For instance, think of the detrimental impact of women taking career breaks on their pensions, for example. You don't always think about that when you are a young woman."

Don't Choose a Dinosaur as a Partner

To juggle the complexities of having a career and raising a family, support is essential. Louise knows from her own experience how important it is to be – and feel – supported from an early age. But it doesn't stop there. Keeping a balance between personal and professional life is never easy – "It is tough. It is still tough" – even if she is positive that things are evolving.

For Louise, the choice of the right partner is an essential component that can determine the chances women have of achieving their professional aspirations. For this reason, she whole-heartedly advises: "Don't marry a dinosaur! Because it can make life very difficult for you." Having just celebrated 30 years of marriage, Louise feels happy she made the right choice. Her husband has been a "tower of strength and a powerful sounding board" for her: "I've always had fantastic support from my husband who has supported me in a professional and personal way. If I hadn't had that, it would have made it even harder for me."

Don't marry a dinosaur! Because it can make life very difficult for you

Working Less yet Being Present

Not working was never an option for Louise. When her children were younger, Louise decided to work part-time for ten years: "That, in some respect, made the whole managing of the work-life balance easier since you could ring-fence yourself sometimes by saying 'I'm not going to be in the office today.'" On the other hand, Louise remembers that she felt like she was doing a full-time job while being paid for half-time, a common story among women in similar situations. Hence, her advice for young women who opt for part-time and still want to advance their career is the following: "If you are needed in the office to attend a client meeting or an important strategic discussion, you have to be there. You have to be flexible enough to address what the professional concerns are." On the other hand, Louise insists that women who have taken the decision to go part-time should embrace it very consciously. The most important thing, she stresses, is "not to feel guilty, not be apologetic, but instead hold on to the decision and focus on where you want to go, and what you want out of your life."

hold on to the decision and focus on where you want to go

Louise is convinced that more awareness, new regulations and creative policies are needed to support and increase the participation of women in the workforce. In particular, these policies should focus on the mid-career period, when women – and also men – struggle with balancing work and family life. For Louise, these policies should be directed at enabling society as a whole to function better and be more inclusive. Employers can do their part, too. In this context, Louise shares the example of her former boss, a man who helped her when her son was born: "My employer said: 'Take as much time off as you want, just come back when you are ready.' Of course, I was very lucky. That makes you feel very supported. But it also makes you feel committed to your boss. My loyalty to my boss and my work increased!"

You Cannot be Liked by Everyone

Once back in the job, whether after a short or longer break, it is essential to be fully committed. And for women, Louise points out, it is particularly important to understand that the professional context is not a competition to be liked by everyone. "It's not a popularity contest, it's about doing the job and doing it well. It doesn't mean to say that you can't have a congenial working environment. But business is business, and as a boss you have to sometimes make decisions which are difficult and unpopular."

The position of a female leader in any professional environment can be challenging. Even in the senior position she holds today, Louise still experiences situations where she is treated differently to her male colleagues: "Less so than when I first started my career, but I still sometimes get some irritating comments from colleagues or business associates. And I am still often the only woman or one of only very few women in the room."

Louise concedes that these negative or misplaced comments are not necessarily deliberate, but rather the result of the unconscious bias that still prevails. Her way to respond to such situations is to be self-aware, assertive and know that all people are biased: "We all have it, I have it as well." In this way, it is possible to react to sexist remarks and attitudes in a "firm and business-like style and to push back in a way that nicely puts interlocutors in their place without being offensive." Louise is convinced that an emphatic attitude is also part of her personal recipe for success: "You have to be prepared to work hard, you've got to be fearless. You have to have a relatively thick skin and be prepared to let things pass if people disagree with you." She says that the sooner women develop a "who cares?" attitude, the better. In practice, "this means stopping giving too much importance to what others think about what you should be doing and focusing on life's fundamentals: health, family, personal relations and any other things that are important to you."

the sooner women develop a "who cares?" attitude, the better

Juggling Family and Career

Can women have both a professional life and a rich family life? For Louise, the answer is clear: yes, it is possible, just as it was for her. Louise got married at the age of 33 – late by the standards of the time. When she made that decision, Louise refused to make a choice between having a demanding professional career and nurturing a family. But, Louise concedes, it must be clear to every woman that achieving this is not easy. There will always be periods where balancing the two is difficult, especially when children are younger. There will always be situations where women "feel that they are not doing either thing to the best of their ability," and there is the guilt. Today, Louise proudly says that her children are her biggest achievement in life: "Bringing up two children who are proving to be successful in their own right, and who are happy, is the most important thing." Louise realised that she needed to address things differently with each of her kids, a son and a daughter. Mothers of sons, she explains, have a big responsibility to make them understand that women are equal and how they can best support women: "They pave the way for their boys' future relationships." While with boys the relationship "feels more educational", with daughters it feels "more like solidarity and also encouragement, as my mother did with me: Always be independent, always be able to support yourself."

The Challenge of a Leader is to Let Others Grow

For Louise, the main qualities of any good leader are easy to describe: clarity, good communication, the ability to listen. When asked about differences in male and female leadership styles, Louise concedes that it is difficult to make generalisations. However, she sees certain trends: "Quite often you see men who are much more prepared to lead from the front, to be out there." Women, on the other hand, tend to be more "collaborative and consensual, wanting to take people with them."

Louise describes her own leadership style as a very direct one that can sometimes appear intimidating – "but when you know me, you know that the door is always open." Louise is a leader who values other people's opinions, and takes them into account; and a leader whose own leadership style continues to evolve, as she has changed positions in her company, moving from hands-on positions to more strategic and "ambassadorial" roles. Every time, there are opportunities and challenges. One of the most important is allowing others to grow on their own: "It is hard to let go. You've done some things; there have been your pet project or your client. It is actually quite hard to say to someone else: you can do this, you can run it. Because I am going off to do something different now." This is especially difficult when "with your experience you can quite see how it ought to be done."

Brussels is a Welcoming Place for Women

For Louise, Brussels is a special place, a unique power hub. The city's decision-making processes depend on complex collaborative and consensual ways of doing things. As a consequence, even public relations consultancies in Brussels are much less competitive than they would usually be in places like the US or the UK: "Here we are used to working alongside each other, realising that sometimes there needs to be some sort of negotiation or accommodation if we want to get to a certain position." What adds to this special atmosphere is the fact that people in Brussels "are used to working with people of different nationalities, with different interests, business interests, political persuasions. They sort of crunch it all together to come up with an agreed position, a common stance."

Louise, a businesswoman who has worked all over the world, considers the Brussels atmosphere particularly welcoming for women. Many of the leading consulting firms in Brussels are in fact run by women and there are role models to whom younger women can turn for inspiration: "These are all women who have made it to the top in the consultancy profession and there's no reason why more shouldn't be following in their footsteps."

We Need More Everyday "He-for-She"

Louise admits that female networking groups were very important and useful for her: "They do a great job in helping women meet each other, sharing experiences and ways to tackle challenges." But nowadays, in order to increase female participation in the workplace, engaging men is crucial: reaching out to men, including them and getting them on board, letting them be ambassadors for gender diversity: "They could help carry the torch forward. We should enable them to do that." Louise wonders whether the time for exclusively female networking has gone and women need to revise their strategy to bring about change: "Maybe we needed these female networking groups to start with, and we may still need them. But beyond that we need more of this he-for-she stuff" (a reference to the HeForShe campaign initiated by UN Women). Men need to engage in diversity discussions, including around gender but going beyond this too.

When Louise's company engages in female networking activities, they try to do more than "just" networking events. They meet to discuss concrete professional development or a policy matter. Louise further points out that it is crucial to have the "right culture" in the company. As with many other businesses, her own company FTI faces the challenge of seeing women leave in the middle stages of their careers. This is being addressed by the company but also needs to be tackled by accompanying government-led policy frameworks that address issues such as parental leave.

Another barrier to overcome is the bias against older women. Louise is convinced that women are still viewed differently from men when it comes to age. She speaks of the repeated occasions on which she has heard questions such as "When are you finally going to retire and spend time with your grand-children?" from male and sometimes female interlocutors. Once again, Louise does not accept being told what she is expected to do:

"Bloody hell, I'm not going to be pensioned off. If you still have something to contribute and the energy to go ahead, it is your responsibility to continue. Go for it!"

Flexibility, Quotas and Encouragement

What works for Louise is to have an approach that is results-oriented. Flexible working hours is an essential strategy that benefits both men and women: "It is more important to be judged on the basis of performance, output and results, rather than on the basis of being in the office." Another winning strategy is quotas and targets. Like so many other senior women, her mindset has changed over the years: "If ten years ago you had said to me 'What do you think of quotas for women on boards?' I would have probably said: 'No, people must advance on the basis of their performance.' Now I think what is disappointing is how slowly things are moving."

Finally, Louise insists that women need to help and encourage other women. This solidarity is key to continue opening the way. To illustrate how important that can be, she tells a story from her time as a young diplomat: "I had just arrived at Kuala Lumpur and was invited by our High Commissioner to dinner. There was a huge table with about 25 people. And there was this formidable wife of the High Commissioner, and she was very educated and extremely scary to me. She used to smoke cigars. We come to the end of this dinner, and there are all these international diplomats around the table and she says: 'Right, ladies, shall we withdraw?' But then she sort of barked across the table: 'Not you, Louise, you are here in your own right!' You know what a boost that was for me? I stayed with the men and the cigars, talking about Malaysian politics, and she led all the ladies out. Women like that help to make a difference!"

Not you, Louise, you are here in your own right!

But Louise also warns that sometimes there are surprises on the path towards gender equality, and tells a story from her first visit to Madagascar as a young diplomat. On the first evening, when she was about to go to sleep, the reception called her and a male voice asked: "Ma'am, will you be wanting a man for the night?" Today's Louise laughs as she concludes: "When you ask to be treated equally, be ready for awkward situations."

Wisdom, Tips, Dos & Don'ts for a Woman Leader-to-be

Know what you want to **achieve** in your life and **develop a strategy** to get there.

Do not feel **guilty** about children or work but show up for the important stuff.

Approach your professional development in a strategic way. Find a **mentor**.

Don't worry about what **other people** think or say. Get on with what you need to do in life.

Leadership is about **delegating**. Let go of pet projects.

Danuta Hübner

Polish. Member of the European Parliament, former European Commissioner. The woman economist who worked on getting Poland into the EU.

Many Snowflakes Can Stop the Traffic

Poland Unfolding

As a young girl, Danuta Hübner had different interests to most girls her age, learning English with a pen friend in the West. Today, she retains the inquiring mind of a young woman. With a mix of tough determination, an air of wisdom and a generous spirit, Danuta speaks of her career as a gradual process without particular role models. Equipped with an interest in the world, ambition, determination and the courage to change things, Danuta found herself on several occasions the person with the right skills and knowledge, in the right place at the right time.

Danuta grew up in communist Poland, a society characterised by economic and political struggle, repression and some reform efforts. She studied economics in Warsaw and taught for many years at a university. Danuta's career took a change of direction when she entered government: "When the change in Poland came, I was ready to get involved because I was prepared. I had skills and abilities that were needed, so when I was called and asked if I would join the government, I said yes." She knew about economics and strategic planning and had a vision for Poland.

Danuta describes herself as a person who focuses on possibilities, not on difficulties. She found herself in "impossible" situations: "When I became the chief negotiator for the accession of Poland to the OECD, in the mid-90s, other countries like Hungary or the Czech Republic were very advanced and about to join. Poland was nowhere and nobody saw the accession as feasible. Then the Prime Minister asked who would do it and nobody replied. So I thought: I will! And I did it. We did it in two years." She also led the preparations for the accession of Poland to the EU, as Secretary of State and then Minister for European Affairs.

Persistence during Struggle

As one of the few people in Poland who knew and understood how the European Union worked, Danuta quickly built up experience within government and then at the multilateral level. First, she held various high-level positions within the Polish government, such as Under Secretary of State in the Ministry of Industry and Trade, Secretary of State, Advisor to the President and Minister. In Brussels, Danuta was the Polish member of the Convention on the Future of Europe, and later became EU Commissioner for Regional Policy (2004-2009). Since then, Danuta has been a Member of the European Parliament. Because of her knowledge of European affairs, she was an obvious choice: "Clearly, I could say 'no' to my political colleagues. I could have been afraid of the challenge, but I was not."

Whilst Danuta's career has not been without considerable tough struggles, she has enjoyed the support of mentors or allies in academia as well as politics. Having grown up under a communist regime that expected women to work, yet also upheld traditional roles at home, her family was equally supportive: "It was always my decision to work but I was encouraged in the sense that the women in my family were proud of me."

Opposition and barriers made Danuta resilient and able to resist pessimism: "Normally those people who see problems and difficulties first don't act … but I was always like Tom the cat (from Tom and Jerry, the American animated series). I'm the type of person who doesn't see the potential failure of something that I am undertaking. That helps a lot."

Where are the Women?

Danuta talks of gender discrimination as a "permanent element of our landscape in Europe, in every aspect of our lives, and in all institutions". She observes the pervasive bias still present, for example, in the European Parliament, where female MEPs are still not as recognised and respected as male MEPs. For her, the situation is still "painful" to observe.

she was frequently called Danusha (a childish diminutive) by her peers in government

Danuta believes that both men and women question women's authority more often than men's, and doubt women's competence. This is reflected in salary and promotion patterns, public positions, language, family life patterns, etc. Often, these double standards are expressed in subtle ways that cannot be easily explained and that makes them even more difficult to address. For example, Danuta recalls that she was frequently called Danusha (a childish diminutive) by her peers in government. In TV debates, while men were addressed by their titles as ministers or doctors, Danuta was addressed simply as Mrs. It was only through living in the US for a period that she came to realise that this treatment was condescending and patronising: "Women should not accept being downgraded". Since then, she demands the same treatment as her male peers by speaking up and drawing attention to the biases.

Personal and Professional Lives

Danuta explains that for her being a professional and having a personal life is very difficult: "There are women who do not want to have professional lives and they are happy. But I think most women just want to have the freedom to choose." As a result, she advocates public policies which offer women the choice to do what they want and combine the different spheres of their lives. Danuta recognises that she is from an earlier generation, which meant she could not necessarily rely on a strong partner at home to help with family tasks. As she says of her husband: "It was much easier to reach out to the grandmothers for help than to share work at home. He would never refuse to do so. But he didn't always realise that it was needed. We were still of a generation that was overwhelmed by tradition, strongly influenced by the church, by traditional perceptions of women and men in the family but also in public life." In Central and Eastern European countries, more changes in societies and politicians are needed to create conditions so that women there can "have it all".

The Need for a Critical Mass of People

We are not effective if we are alone ... but many snowflakes can stop the traffic

Danuta mentions repeatedly that she does not believe in individual actions: "We are all so inter-related". To change the current gender imbalance, the sine qua non strategy is more collaboration among women: "We are not effective if we are alone. Women are like snowflakes: if you are alone you dissolve when the temperature changes, but many snowflakes can stop the traffic. To bring about a change, we should be aware of this!"

You Have to Feel that You Can Change the World

Danuta's wish to change the world was her biggest driver: her capacity to see reality with a critical eye and realise there are things that must be changed, and her openness to acquiring new professional skills and continuing to learn and challenge herself. For her, fundamental factors for successful leadership in today's world are the capacity to communicate by showing passion and by convincing others, and the ability to compromise and negotiate consensus. According to Danuta, a good leader is someone with the passion and the capacity to create collective ownership around a cause. Moreover, a good leader is someone with the courage to tell people that what they need is perhaps something different from what they want. It is someone who is ready to lose elections to focus on a long-term vision. In order to achieve this, a leader needs to be sure of their own strength. As Danuta states: "You have to be aware of your individual role and contribution, that you have a vision and you want to do something with it."

The Need to Work Together and Learn and Adapt

Danuta contends that the image of leadership has been largely dominated by male stereotypes and interpretations: leaders should be tall, loud and confident. But Danuta emphasises that today's world calls for a different set of leadership skills – skills that many women already demonstrate: "I'm surprised that we see so few women in leadership today, because the leadership we need today must be based on getting people to solve challenges, on being more consensual, collaborative and open to others' views." While men are often quick to assume that the only path is the one they have chosen, women are generally less hierarchical in the way they approach challenges, more open to asking questions and hearing others' opinions.

Danuta's own experience has shown her that combined efforts brings better results than an individual approach. "We (women) are generally much more oriented towards getting together around the fire and thinking and talking and acting together." And Danuta firmly believes that the interconnected, transnational complex challenges Europe and the world are currently facing – climate change, economic crisis, internal EU difficulties, border security, refugees, etc. – demand this kind of leadership.

Invest in Learning

Danuta describes herself as a collaborative leader who has become more assertive and empathetic with experience. She highlights that it remains important to her to develop real substantive competences instead of just being good at politics. That is why she always continues to invest in learning. As she says: "With time, you don't spend so much time on issues on which you spent a lot of time years ago. You learn to adapt faster to the different challenges and contexts: It's something different to be a Commissioner or a Minister or even a Parliamentarian. As a Minister or Commissioner, you have to bite your tongue much more often as you try to convince others to act, because there are so many interests around. If you want to be effective, you have to play your games differently politically while maintaining your honesty."

Life is Not Just about One Big Accomplishment

Like many women, Danuta is very proud of her family and particularly of her daughters. However, she also feels a deep sense of achievement over bringing her country into the European Union and working towards improving Poland's image in Europe as well as the role of Poland within the Union. "It was very important for me to get Poland into it and then convince Europe and the world that Poland and the Poles feel responsible for Europe, that we are committed and understand the problems we want to contribute to solving." She sees it as a major team accomplishment.

The Richness of Brussels

In a way, Brussels exemplifies Danuta's credo for collaboration. The diversity of the city is the essence of what is being done here, "bringing everybody together and trying to build unity", as she puts it. As Danuta tells it, while the Scandinavians brought human rights and democracy debates, the countries from Central and Eastern Europe brought a belief that "everything is possible" because they had gone through "impossible" transitions.

The European Parliament is a good example of this approach of hosting diverse people under one roof, allowing for differences and enabling compromise: "Each time we start a discussion, we start from radically different positions. Then we know that we will only be successful if we find a compromise."

We have a rhetoric of equality and human rights, but it is a permanent fight

Living in this culture of compromise-building and accommodating everybody's perspectives is not simple and it does not always bring the best results, but that is the European reality. Danuta argues that it is very important for European citizens to physically travel to Brussels: "As members of the European Parliament we can bring people to Brussels. If you don't come, and you don't touch it with your own hands, you will never develop this feeling of belonging to something which shares a common responsibility. So Brussels is, indeed, very special."

Nonetheless, Brussels can also be hypocritical, especially towards women: "We have a rhetoric of equality and human rights, but it is a permanent fight. Brussels does not always give the same opportunities to men and women." According to Danuta, Brussels' power dynamics are the result of what happens at the member state level, where formally there are equal opportunities, but education and policies still entrench de facto gender bias. "The problem with gender equality is that we talk, talk, and talk. But we don't see results."

She would like to see the work of advancing women being done on the national level, by political parties establishing quotas for women, and by civil society giving more visibility to the achievements of women. Moreover, the educational systems in member states should play their part in making young girls open to the possibility of political engagement at the European level. And Danuta agrees that men should be engaged in this process, formally and informally.

Wisdom, Tips, Dos & Don'ts for Women Leaders-to-be

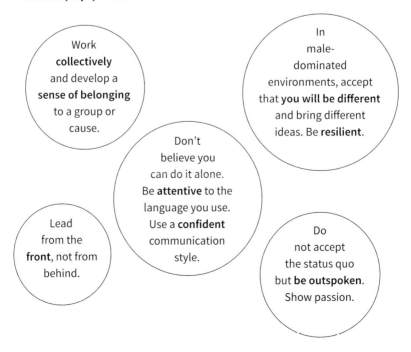

Work **collectively** and develop a **sense of belonging** to a group or cause.

In male-dominated environments, accept that **you will be different** and bring different ideas. Be **resilient**.

Don't believe you can do it alone. Be **attentive** to the language you use. Use a **confident** communication style.

Lead from the **front**, not from behind.

Do not accept the status quo but **be outspoken**. Show passion.

Lotte Leicht

Danish. Director of Human Rights Watch Brussels Office. A lawyer with an intense sense of mission who dedicates her life to defending and promoting human rights and freedom around the world.

Success is Something You Achieve with Others

Finding a Mission

Becoming an international human rights lawyer was a natural progression for Lotte. She grew up in a household with frequent debates on politics and world affairs: "We always had many people in the house. They thought we were fighting, but we really liked to discuss! It sounded very dramatic but it wasn't. It was because we all wanted to get our views across." While she was interested in politics, Lotte realised that party politics were not for her because she could not figure out what party she would join, and she did not like the idea of being put into a specific "box". She rather wanted to work across groups and factions: "It was logical for me to become engaged in cross-party issues and try to foster coalitions around projects instead."

Not immediately knowing what to do after she finished high school, Lotte became a ski instructor. After two years, Lotte decided to study law. Whilst at law school, Lotte became fascinated by international humanitarian law, a rather "exotic" field at the time. Lotte was fortunate enough to find like-minded university colleagues and progressive professors, who shared her passion. Thanks to these and other visionaries, the new field of study of international humanitarian law took off in Denmark and led to the founding of the Danish Centre for Human Rights (now known as the Danish Institute for Human Rights). Lotte worked there as a volunteer for a while and at some point – still as a student – went to the head of the centre and asked him to give her a job, saying: "I'm a good student, I'm spending a lot of time in this place." But, she continues, "he didn't have any funds to give me a job, so I had to go out and work in a law firm as a student, just to make my way. But after three months in the law firm, he called me and said 'I think I have a job for you'". This was a pivotal moment: Lotte got to work on a large East-West Conference – a forum for political discussions among dissidents from Eastern Europe. She was inspired by the atmosphere, by the passion and commitment of the participants. She became active in the new context of the political transformation in Eastern Europe. "This was 1989. And I thought it was fascinating, because it was clear that something was happening but nobody knew exactly what. It was still unclear where it would go and what would happen." Lotte went to work for the International Helsinki Federation for Human Rights in Vienna in 1990, when she was in her mid-twenties. As she recalls: "It was such a privilege. I got thrown into meetings. I met all of these extraordinary people, many of them ended up as ministers and presidents."

It was while with the Helsinki Federation that Lotte learnt to mobilise ministries and reach out to journalists to raise awareness and generate pressure: "The first time I spoke to Václav Havel (writer, political dissident, first president of the Czech Republic, 1993-2003) he was in jail. He called me and said 'Look, you've got to help us'. I was sitting in the office as a young law student – though I was no longer a student, I still felt like one!—and I got on the phone. You call ministries, you call journalists, you whip up support, and it becomes a goal in and of itself just to get someone out of jail – again, again, again, again..."

The people Lotte worked with on these struggles were her inspiration: "They were amazing people. The ones who really have impressed me are the ordinary people who become extraordinary in extraordinary situations. In wars, you see the worst in people, the worst of what people can do to each other. But you also see the other extreme. You really meet extraordinary people who have no names in press stories but are simply amazing." One person stands out in particular as a role model and mentor: Alison Des Forges, an American historian and human rights activist who specialised in the African Great Lakes region, particularly the 1994 Rwandan Genocide, and who died in an air crash in 2009. Lotte worked with Alison when she set up the Human Rights Watch (HRW) office in Brussels in 1994. Lotte was impressed by Alison's attempts to save friends and colleagues who had worked for HRW when the genocide started: "She was tiny but tough as a nut. I was the clumsy tall girl beside her." Alison taught Lotte many lessons, including that in anything one does, what matters most are the people. And that, in diplomatic terms, "You should always walk into a meeting knowing more than the people you meet with. You have to prepare yourself."

Lotte's work requires resilience as it often means hearing about atrocities and loss and raising awareness and attention about it. She considers herself fortunate because her family and friends provide her with a web of support that sustains her. She has known many friends a very long time, and many have professions that keep them busy or take them to other parts of the world. Yet, in times of need, Lotte can rely on them: "It doesn't matter where I travel, there is always someone I know."

Are Women Still Only a Ray of Colour in a Picture of Men in Dark Suits?

Lotte often found herself in professional situations where she was the only woman or one of just a few. She says she was not directly discriminated against but found herself changing her behaviour to adapt to a male-only context. For example, in some discussions, Lotte avoided using terms such as "feminist" as she felt their use would be counter-productive in the broader human rights context: "It is becoming more okay now, but being a feminist was sort of an accusation, like you are just a crazy person." In other situations, such as within her own organisation, Lotte did refer to herself as a feminist when talking to men, telling them: "Of course I am a feminist, and so should you be. You have daughters, or sisters, or female friends. You want something good for them. You want equal access and equal treatment, no?"

However, Lotte continues to see Brussels and the field of humanitarian law as a man's world. And she is greatly concerned that women continue to be mostly seen by society in the context of the family whereas men are identified by their professions: "There are far more men with feminist views nowadays, who take for granted that people should be treated equally and with respect. But still, there are always far fewer women than men in the meeting rooms in Brussels. In photos, the few women stand out because of their colourful clothes in group photos of men all dressed in dark suits. And that has not changed."

Of course I am a feminist, and so should you be. You have daughters, or sisters, or female friends

Also, in terms of influence and access to power, the reality remains very male-controlled: "In the little red book of phone numbers, it is very often the man who knows the man." While Lotte does not necessarily insist there should be 50-50 gender parity in decision-making, she believes that having too many male-dominated environments is a problem. She agrees with Hillary Clinton's remark that "women are the world's biggest untapped resource". As Lotte puts it: "Many women are still disadvantaged by not being included, showing their potential and contributing their views to important discussions. That is really a pity because we are missing out on these voices, these talents and a range of views. Women's absence from the table directly affects the outcome – and therefore the success – of the discussions."

From "Can Women Have it All?" to "Can WE Have it All?"

Lotte has a long-term partner and does not have children. She says that at some point she made a choice not to have children. Still, she says: "I am probably a 'sad' example of a woman that didn't have it all. I think I am proof that if I had wanted to have it all, it would probably have been difficult. The tendency still is that men can have it all, they have one job – the job outside the house. Women have, God knows, how many jobs…" Lotte would like to see mentalities changing in such a way that "having it all" is no longer a question for women alone: "We have to get away from that question. Now it is about whether a man and a woman can have it all." This means finding practical solutions that allow both to pursue careers and have a family. Lotte does not now regret her decision not to have children as her life has always been full of enriching experiences, but she does admit that the question was an issue in the years when she had to choose. "I decided that I would rather spend my second phase of adult life doing things other than being a mother. And that was a choice – a personal choice. It was not something that had to do with work."

Being Part of Something Larger

Lotte is proud of having been part of the group that was instrumental in setting international standards around human rights: "I was part of a group of lawyers who documented the first cases of human rights abuses in the former Yugoslavia, in a way that they could stand up to scrutiny in court." Advocating for transitional justice and an International Criminal Court (ICC) made clear that future atrocities would come with consequences, and sent a strong message that impunity would not prevail: "A united front of many organisations – victims' groups, non-governmental groups, diplomats, politicians, governments, and international organisations." This coalition of actors had a common mission: they all wanted to take justice forward and "raise the price" of crimes. For Lotte it was "the realisation that if you want to achieve big things, you have to work with everyone. The more different parts of society are part of an initiative, the better." Other success stories have followed: standard-setting regarding war atrocities including landmines, cluster munitions, child soldiers, etc. However, it remains difficult to see the standards upheld in reality: "with successes come the failures, because the implementation phase is really hard. It's always a bumpy road, up and down. As human rights advocates, we have to focus on the long game."

Her professional successes are the achievements she accomplished with others. Not being afraid to try, not being afraid of failure are crucial for her. She considers remaining creative (about how to achieve things) to be vital, as she does not believe there is just one way for someone to succeed at something.

From Knowing it All to Listening to Others

Lotte has worked with numerous leaders and in many situations. She defines good leadership as being when someone leads by example, is respectful towards others, and is willing to listen and learn. Moreover, for Lotte a leader is someone who accepts limits, and knows s/he cannot achieve results alone: "it is not a one-woman or one-man show. It is about persuading others to come with you and to be part of your success, and to be proud of it. You would be surprised how proud people are when they are part of making a difference. It is a very human trait to actually want to do something good." Good leadership is also about recognising the group's effort: "Do not take all the credit yourself. Really know that you have a team working with you, and recognise it. People get uplifted and inspired if they receive praise and encouragement for the wonderful and smart things they do."

You would be surprised how proud people are when they are part of making a difference

Lotte does, though, acknowledge the bias in the perception of leadership qualities in men and women and how it plays out in language and attitudes. For example, while words such as "determined" have a positive quality when associated with a man (he knows what he wants), the same words often are seen as having negative connotations when associated with a woman (she is insistent, pushy, demanding).

Lotte's own take on leadership also includes the ability to acknowledge one's mistakes. She admits that she has learnt by doing; initially she was fresh and bold, trying to push through her ideas, thinking she knew it all. With time, Lotte has realised that she doesn't know it all and has learnt to adopt more of a listening mode, to reflect more, learn from other people and her own mistakes, be honest and accept her own limits: "If I make a mistake, I am willing to admit that and say 'I'm sorry, I was wrong'. I don't think that makes me a bad leader or a person who my team would not want to work with. I have a feeling they respect that. No one is right all the time…"

Brussels as a Place that Holds Things Together

To make it in this city, you need to be persistent, says Lotte. She describes Brussels as a dynamic place that creates room for newcomers and for new ideas: "In the beginning I was the one running around, knocking on doors: saying 'please listen to me, I have something important to say'. Now, I still do that if I have to. But it is also the other way around: those in power come to you because they know that you have information they need to make important decisions, but also because you have good ideas about what can be done, based on on-the-ground intelligence that others wouldn't have." Brussels is the kind of place where everything tends to come together, and to which people often return. It is also a fluid place where people come and go.

So, according to Lotte, there is a tendency to refer and connect people and recommend those who are good sources of data and expertise. This happens both within the NGO world and among the different Brussels institutions and stakeholders: "I sort of see myself as a big matchmaker, getting people together. I think that is something I really learned from coming to this place. I have not seen that in New York, not in the same way."

Brussels is the place where, in the EU context, 28 countries come together to agree on common positions. So for Lotte, in this city you have to be a good negotiator, and be willing to think in terms of compromise, something that according to her,

I sort of see myself as a big matchmaker

women can do well. However, "you have to make clear to yourself where compromise becomes so watered down that it is no longer worth even going further with an idea." What she sees as problematic about Brussels is the lack of transparency in reaching the compromise: "You hear about decisions once they have been made. But we don't really know how they came to be. Think about this: as Europeans, we have never, ever, seen twenty-eight ministers debate with each other."

Because of this lack of communication between decision-makers and citizens, Brussels is an elitist place, according to Lotte, which top level people come to on a monthly basis, as government leaders or ministers – and in that sense, Brussels is still disconnected from European citizens and the broader world. "Europe needs far more transparency and accountability about how decisions are made." Lotte believes that decision-makers should involve European citizens in meetings once in a while and have more open discussions, especially on tough issues such as refugees, migration and involvement in conflicts abroad that divide public opinion as well as the member states: "I do think that if the ministers around the table knew that there was a camera, they might be saying more thoughtful things than those I hear some of them saying (in private)". She misses seeing a European leader with the capacity to persuade citizens and capture them with a united vision.

Brussels allows motivated people who work hard, get things done and lead through persuasion and win-win consensus to get results. Moreover, Lotte believes that women are really quite good at supporting each other in Brussels: "This is a tough place, but it's also a good place because there is good support, from strong networks."

Gender in the NGO Sector

Talking about gender discrimination in Lotte's line of work can be uncomfortable because human rights are universal and all-inclusive by definition. Human rights entail multiple types of rights and stakeholders. The gender dimension is just one aspect, but it is cross-cutting and hence a widely recognised area in international law and conventions. Because of the fact that educated, smart women lose out along their professional journey, according to Lotte, men need to be part of the effort to change the situation and achieve greater gender parity: "we need to persuade our husbands, our friends, our sons, our brothers that they need to be part of improving the situation. That we're equal to them, and that they need to be speaking for us in their different ways. We have to penetrate male networks and make clear that we need to be a part of them."

Lotte argues in favour of quotas as she sees them as necessary to compel people to move away from traditional mindsets. She also feels that preferential treatment for women is warranted in situations where there are two equally qualified candidates, in order to eventually increase diversity at the higher level. She references the new feminist foreign policy in Sweden, driven by an innovative approach to external politics, which at least in theory provides a new rhetoric for men and women to subscribe to. She would like to see the EU foreign policy adopt a feminist foreign policy approach.

In her own professional environment, Human Rights Watch tried to mainstream gender equality within its own activities as well as structures and human resources. Despite high levels of awareness and constant debate, the staff realised that in order to achieve success they needed a dedicated unit dealing with gender; a unit including gender experts, but also executives, in order to ensure that its directives were enforced and replicated by others in the organisation. For Lotte, it is crucial that executive leadership is fully engaged in raising awareness of gender inequality and changing mentalities. If it is difficult for a human rights organisation like Human Rights Watch to mainstream and enforce gender parity, then "you can only imagine how it is in the sectors where human rights is not part of what you do", says Lotte. This is a lesson learnt that she shares with many interlocutors: "You believe you can mainstream? I don't believe it for a second. Without dedicated leadership which provides the impetus to include this topic in the debate, in the decisions, in the work you do, it won't work."

Wisdom, Tips, Dos & Don'ts for a Woman Leader-to-be

Give **praise and encouragement** generously – to those below, sideways and above you.

Be **conscious** about all your life **choices**.

Focus on the **long game**; you want to influence, succeed and make a difference for a long time.

Sustain **friendships** through work and through life.

Be **your kind** of feminist.

Isabella Lenarduzzi

Belgian/Italian. Social Entrepreneur, founder and Director of JUMP. A pioneer of gender equality in Belgium.

If Nothing is Changing, Make the Changes Yourself

A Symbol of Female Power and Assertiveness

"It is the first time in history that women have the right and ability to create their own lives, following their own personality, developing their own skills and talents, really choosing their lives. So we have to celebrate that!" So says Isabella Lenarduzzi, the founder of JUMP, a social enterprise that promotes gender equality in the workplace. Isabella chose the colour pink for JUMP's visual identity to emphasise the power that lies in women.

Born in Brussels to Italian parents and raised speaking three languages in the cosmopolitan atmosphere of the city, Isabella embodies the internationally-minded citizen of the EU capital. In 2006, Isabella launched JUMP in Brussels, and she now manages 3 companies, one NGO and a team of 12 people with offices in Brussels and Paris. As a public figure in Belgium, Isabella is frequently invited to public debates and brings a feminist perspective to the news on radio and TV. She has received awards for her engagement, including winner of "Women Inspiring Europe" from the European Institute for Gender Equality and the "Femme d'Exception" from the Belgian Minister for Equal Opportunities.

Finding her Mission through Life's Shocks

Before discovering her true mission to advance the professional prospects of women, Isabella went through a number of key experiences, or "shocks", as she refers to them. These experiences helped Isabella to become aware of the need to change the way the professional world perceives and deals with women.

Her first key experience dates back to the early 1990s. Together with her two male business partners, Isabella was about to sell her company, an enterprise that organised student fairs in various European countries. The buyers were also men, and treated her differently to her two male partners: "I was considered by the buyers as the personal assistant of my two male partners. This devaluing of my role was not because I was Isabella Lenarduzzi; it was because I was a woman." Disheartened, she soon left the company. Subsequently she followed her husband to Italy, set up a consultancy and worked as Deputy Director of the Naples Science Museum.

Moving to the south of Italy was the second shock. There, Isabella was confronted with a "strong patriarchal culture", a culture that was much more openly sexist than what she had previously encountered. "I learnt that a woman wasn't really considered anybody unless she was the spouse or daughter of a man. A woman didn't really have an identity herself."

A few years later she returned to Brussels with her young children, after having gone through a difficult divorce. There, Isabella organised a series of business events and created the "Brussels Job Days" for the Brussels Chamber of Commerce, a new event concept for on-site job interviews. But Isabella was dismayed to see that the situation for women had not advanced in the 8 years since she left – it was her third shock: "Nothing had changed. There were no events, there was no media speaking about women, except about their beauty, their well-being, their fashion, but not their autonomy." Isabella was convinced that, for women, autonomy results from a paid job, through a real career where women can bring in their skills and talents. For her, this "aha" moment was the turning point: "I said to myself: since nothing has changed since I left Belgium, I will create it myself." So she went on to set up JUMP, which today is a leading social enterprise working with organisations and individuals to close the gap between women and men at work.

I said to myself: since nothing has changed since I left Belgium, I will create it myself

Making Change

Since she was young Isabella has felt a strong desire to help change society for the better, getting involved in initiatives to fight against racism and violence, for instance. The inspiration to become a change-maker came from her father: "My father was the creator of the Erasmus Programme (a European scheme to support the international mobility of university students, established in 1987), and I saw in him a man full of ambition. Even if he is a person in a wheelchair, and even if he has had difficulties, he never said 'This is impossible for me, this is impossible for Europe.' He had a mission in life, and I always felt I had a mission in life, too. Thanks to the energy and the bravery that I learned from him, I could face any obstacles and go on." Isabella is driven by the conviction that women who "feel their power, their power to change things, their power to be themselves can change not only their families, but also the place where they work, their company and their societies." Isabella has therefore focused over the last few years on helping companies to change towards that end and to be more gender-inclusive. Her credo is that this will help to make the economy work in a different way – which will, ultimately, create a better world.

Beyond the "I'm No Good" and "I Have to Please Everybody" Mindsets

Developing your own way of leading is a long process. As part of it, Isabella believes that it is crucial to recognise what the barriers are, including doubts within yourself as well as external obstacles. Isabella reflects that receiving criticism from others initially made her feel inferior and inadequate. She then found ways to deal with such criticism, including where relevant through seeking appropriate training. So she has learned how, in her moments of doubt, to react and overcome the problem.

Isabella also underlines the importance of being able to recognise gender stereotypes and learn how to deal with them: "We need to understand the kind of environment we are operating in, in order to be kind to ourselves from time to time

We need to enable other women to be authentic

and also to enable other women to be authentic and not feel the need to wear men's suits and act like men." Getting past the pressure to be perfect all the time, to please everybody – including your own exaggerated and unrealistic demands – and to always do what your environment and society expects you to do is an essential piece of the puzzle of becoming a leader: "We expect from women – from ourselves too – that they are exceptional. The best, all the time. We don't let them have a small defect or lack a skill. They always need to be excellent and perform more than 100%; they need to be 150%. This is exhausting. So when you are aware of this expectation both on yourself and on other women, you are able to better respond to it. Instead of trying to achieve this unrealistic perfection all the time, we should work on realising and seeing more clearly how we are doing and appreciate our efforts and results and the efforts and results of other women. I have the sense that most women leaders are actually doing much better than we think we are doing; we need to see this clearly."

Women are Heroes – but Cannot be Superwomen all the Time

Isabella admits that she does not have a perfect work-life balance, as she works many hours, pursues her passion through her work and gets a lot of energy and satisfaction from it. She believes that choosing the right partner is of major importance for a woman's career. Having a family can be complicated and having a demanding job and a family is usually difficult as well. In order to manage both, to combine both parts – and actually "have it all" – men need to be brought on board and become responsible for the family, too. "Men need to spend more time with family tasks. Women are often heroes but we cannot be superwomen all the time! We really need to share." Isabella underlines the fact that women still take the large bulk of family tasks, even when working full-time. But, as she says: "Isn't it much better to live in couples where both are able to develop themselves, their skills and talents?"

Being Happy is Your Biggest Gift

For Isabella, her biggest accomplishment is having managed to "have it all": a family, a job she enjoys, an immense network, friends, and to make an impact on society. Having achieved all this is a direct result of the many risks Isabella took in the course of her life, not only as an entrepreneur but also at a personal level. Not being afraid to try new things, to change one's life, to embrace new challenges "will make your life exciting and will make you a happy person", says Isabella. And she continues: "I really think that when children have a happy mother, they are happy."

A Good Leader is Authentic – not Male or Female

For Isabella, there is no such thing as male or female leadership styles. She advocates a change from a gendered perspective on leadership (the Think-Leader-Think-Male bias) to an individual one. In order to be a good a leader, "it is important to know yourself and to be authentic, to embrace both your female and male traits." A leader is good and authentic if he or she "has identified his or her femininity and masculinity and has achieved a marriage between them." Isabella says that at the start of her career she over-emphasised the "masculine part" of her leadership – toughness, competitiveness, etc. – since she thought that was what was needed (and expected) in the male-dominated world of business and entrepreneurship. Indeed, Isabella remembers, there was "no soul in my leadership, I didn't respect my femininity". Over time, she worked on reappraising her femininity and the result was neither a female nor a male leadership style – it became *Isabella's* style: "Because what you see is what you get. I am authentic, all the time." Being "just" Isabella entails both her strengths and her weaknesses.

In Brussels You Can Choose Where to Belong

Brussels is "Isabella's city": "It feels like I grew up in the Berlaymont (home of the European Commission). Europe is my home and my identity." For

Isabella, the diversity of this city "requires flexibility, curiosity and open-mindedness".

Isabella stresses that Brussels is a great place to actually live gender equality: "We have so many different communities and cultural backgrounds that life for a woman is easier here than in many other countries. We can choose the environment we want to live in: we can choose a very archaic environment, or we can choose a very progressive environment. And we can choose a partner from all these different kinds of environments and backgrounds because they are all there. So it's a matter of choice and of knowing what you want."

If You Treat a Woman like a Man, You are Holding Her Back

Gender equality is on the EU agenda, not least thanks to the presence of the EU institutions and the fact they theoretically put gender equality upfront. But in Belgium, inequalities prevail and as Isabella says, "the life of a woman is not similar to the life of a man." In these conditions, Isabella argues that men and women should have the same rights while being recognised in their differences: "Women need a different kind of attention from the company. If you treat a woman like a man, you are holding her back." Understanding the differences between men and women when it comes to their additional responsibilities and tasks is "the new challenge employers have to face. They need to be aware of the privileges that men still have." Isabella acknowledges that the new situation – more women in the workplace and in leadership positions – can be frightening for some men: "It's the first time that men need to face this massive competition with women who are as qualified and even more qualified at times. This can be frightening to some men." A way of bringing men on board is to show them that a gender-diverse workplace is a stronger and more innovative environment.

the more you have gender equality targets, the higher the quality of your team

Gender Equality is a Management Issue

"Women represent 60% of the graduates in Europe," recalls Isabella: "That means that women represent the biggest talent pool." She also adds that women are almost half of the workforce and those who decide about 80%

of the purchase of consumer goods, so in today's Europe women "are" the market. Despite this, women represent only 27% of the board members in the biggest companies in Belgium and less than 15% on the executive level – which means that one company out of two doesn't have even one woman on its executive team: "That means that something is going wrong." To change this situation, gender equality needs to be made a strategic priority, Isabella argues. A customised gender equality plan has to be developed and implemented, targeted and based on the real situation in the company or institution. This will benefit everyone, she stresses: "Every piece of research shows that the more you have gender equality targets, the higher the quality of your team and the better the performance of the organisation, because it attracts very high-level women that would never be attracted by this organisation if they didn't implement specific action plans. This automatically raises the level of quality of the whole team." Finally, Isabella underlines the importance of raising the awareness of the top management since "leading by example is fundamental. Top managers are those able to change the corporate culture!" As Isabella maintains: "diversity is counting people that are different, inclusion is making people count."

Wisdom, Tips, Dos & Don'ts for a Leader-to-be

Don't forget: You can **make a difference** every single day!

Show **solidarity** to other women. To succeed, women need the help of men, but **above all** they need the help of other women.

Know yourself, know your **goals**, respect your uniqueness, have **self-confidence** in your inner value.

Do not focus on perfection: **focus** on the very best **you** can be.

Be **authentic**; when you lead be in touch with yourself.

Oana Lungescu

German, born in Romania. NATO Spokesperson. Raised and educated under a Communist regime, Oana is the first woman, the first journalist and the first Eastern European to be in this position.

Do not Take Freedom for Granted

Switching Sides but Remaining a Journalist

Oana carries with her an air of determination and resilience. Her Eastern European background and history is a formative characteristic of who she is – and also provided the support structure that allowed her to get to where she is today. She comes across as a tough and strong person with an incredible drive, yet a gentleness comes out, especially when she speaks of her family and friends.

She is a trained journalist and still considers herself one: "I like to think of myself as still being a journalist and acting as a journalist inside the organisation (NATO) because in order to do my job, I still have to ask very basic questions." She worked at the BBC for 25 years before taking on her current job. She first joined the Romanian Language Service at the BBC in London in 1985, rising through the ranks and becoming deputy head and then editor. From 1997, she was part of the BBC World Service team in Brussels, covering EU and NATO affairs for radio, television and online in several languages as European affairs correspondent. In 2009-2010 she was posted to Berlin. During her time as a journalist, Oana was at the centre of key European and international developments. She covered the Kosovo war and the aftermath of the Bosnia war; she also covered the political debates over Afghanistan and Iraq. She wrote about the fall of the Iron Curtain in Eastern Europe, the introduction of the euro, NATO and EU enlargement and the Treaty of Lisbon.

With so much happening in the world, Oana had not really planned a career switch. It was chance and her reputation as a journalist which took Oana to the leadership role she has today – the first woman to hold the position of principal spokesperson for the North Atlantic Alliance: "I was in Berlin on holiday, eating an ice-cream, and a phone call came from my predecessor asking me, 'Would you be interested in going for this job? We know it will take some time to decide but just please consider it.'" It was not an easy decision because, being a journalist at heart, the idea of switching sides stirred up all sorts of emotions. Besides, Oana loved her work. Working on her own or in small teams, she knew that the new job would come with a huge responsibility: "Leaving journalism is quite a tough decision to make. It is almost like a death in the family. That's how I experienced it."

But in November 2010, intrigued by the new challenge, she took up the post. As NATO spokesperson, Oana provides strategic communication advice to the NATO Secretary General. She coordinates NATO's 24/7 media operations, as well as planning and directing the media aspects of all major NATO events, including summits and ministerial meetings. She also oversees all speeches and publications by the NATO Secretary General and Deputy Secretary General.

A Central and Eastern European Past

Oana studied English and Spanish in Bucharest. Her mother, an ethnic German, had gone to Germany on a rare tourist visa when she turned 50 years old and had not come back. Oana was a perfect target for the Securitate, the Romanian secret police during Ceaușescu's regime. As she revealed in several BBC documentaries, she had been asked to be an informer in exchange for a passport and cancer medication for her father. Oana refused but it had been a very tough experience. Romania's effort to track the lives of its citizens was on a vast scale – there was a permanent fear of what might happen.

> *She was somebody who had the courage to make a leap into the unknown*

It overshadowed the lives of many Romanians and made people like Oana's mother give up everything. She never again saw her husband. Oana was able to join her mother four years later. She has a deep, and touching admiration for her mother and her courage: "She had done it for me and for the family. She was somebody who had the courage to change her life and make a leap into the unknown for the people she loved, and also because she loved freedom." Clearly Oana's own wish for freedom came at a price; from when she arrived in London in the summer of 1985 until December 1989 (when Ceaușescu fell from power) the Romanian secret police continued to monitor her, despite the fact that she had given up her Romanian citizenship in 1985.

A Man's World

Perhaps the hardship of growing up in Romania under Ceaușescu and the different gender relations – traditional gender roles at home, yet with women actively engaged in the workforce – that existed in Central and Eastern Europe prepared Oana for the atmosphere at NATO. By its very nature, the organisation is male-dominated because most diplomats and military people there are men.

But Oana focuses on her work. "What I have found is that people respect professionalism, so I haven't had different treatment because I am a woman. That is not really the difference. I think, perhaps, I have had different treatment sometimes because of my journalistic background."

However, Oana does note that she has received sexist comments and abuse on social media, noting that in the social media sphere in general, the treatment of women is often brutal and insulting. "There is a severe sexism against women in social media, because (trolls) hide behind Twitter or Facebook and it's much easier to (harass). We need to be aware and, as women, we can also support each other in the social media sphere." Oana has developed some coping mechanisms – blocking certain trolls, not providing a response to condescending and sexist remarks online. She sees this as a problem that social media companies and users need to tackle in the long run.

Oana admits that she works hard and has always done so and the working environment of NATO's headquarters is not family-friendly due to the long, intense working hours. "I can't say that I have it all in the conventional sense of the word, because I don't have a family, I don't have children. At NATO, in this particular job, I think it is harder to maintain that balance. But this is my choice and I am quite happy with my choice." Some women at NATO make a different choice to Oana's, but it is difficult.

Leadership is about Respect, Humility and Listening to Others

Being a pragmatist and doer, Oana admits that she has not spent much time thinking about her own leadership, or about leadership in general. She considers respect, humility, the ability to listen, and a focus on results as core features of a leader. This was reflected in her approach during her first few months at NATO, when she faced a steep learning curve and often doubted herself: "There was a lot happening in the world. This meant that I had to learn fast and learn on the job. I was very fortunate to have some great people around me, who supported me and who said 'yes, you can do it', because frankly, I wasn't sure in the first month that I could do it. But I have done it!"

It was a politically tense time – an important NATO summit, the ongoing Afghanistan and Kosovo operations, the rise of a more assertive Russia, as well as a new NATO operation for the protection of Libyan civilians. Oana realised that her skills as a journalist – not being afraid to be in the middle of everything – came in handy, as she had to operate like a "super producer". She had to learn to ensure that all voices were heard, that information was widely shared, that everybody knew their role. "It is like three dimensional chess in a way. It's about being able to have an overview of the whole picture, about coordinating and making sure that everybody knows their role as much as possible, so that NATO's public message reflects the consensus of all 29 allies. It is not easy but it is certainly very rewarding."

While Oana has a direct and focused approach, she describes her manner as tending to be academic at times in the way she deals with colleagues: "I was a teacher in a secondary school in the mountains in Romania quite a few years ago, so perhaps I still carry some of that with me." She fully recognises that she cannot do the job alone and is appreciative of team work.

Good and Bad Leadership vs Male and Female Leadership Styles

Oana prefers to talk about good and bad leadership rather than male and female leadership styles: "I think what matters is to have good leaders. I have had managers or colleagues in positions of responsibility who I thought were very good examples in terms of getting results and also taking their teams with them and being responsible and listening. I would not identify their leadership aptitude or success with gender because I have met some women who are extremely ambitious, very focused on themselves and on their own careers and who made poor leaders."

Emotional Intelligence as a Sine Qua Non for Great Leadership

In her roles as a journalist and now NATO spokesperson, Oana has had the privilege of being close to international leaders, and has come to recognise the importance of emotional intelligence for effective leadership: "I have certainly realised how important the personal relationship between leaders is in achieving results. In many ways, much depends on the ability to relate to somebody else, to focus on them, to listen to their concerns, to see how you can find solutions together. This makes a great leader."

the ability to relate to somebody else, to focus on them … makes a great leader

This sensitivity needs to be paired with a certain boldness and willingness to step forward. "I come from a generation and from a place where we were not supposed to speak up, not just as women but as individuals. So, in a way it was doubly hard to actually break through and be assertive. I can say that I learned assertiveness much later in life than people of my age who grew up in Western Europe. But at the same time, we also had a very strong rebellious streak because of where we came from, because we couldn't take our basic rights for granted. So, those of us who have gone through this are now stronger and perhaps can put things into a broader perspective."

Brussels Rewards Multilingualism and Networking

Oana finds the city of Brussels a very small place. But she also says that "there are many Brussels. There is the European village and there is Brussels itself, with a high rate of unemployment. In many ways, we expatriates do not always see that Brussels. I think it is important that we do, because the world of institutions – be they European institutions or NATO – is not the real Brussels in many ways. But of course, it's an important part of it."

A way to relate more easily to the various institutions is by staying in touch with people as they change jobs and at times move between institutions and reach more senior postings. "We had a dinner for instance not so long ago with colleagues from the EU and I realised I knew most of them from my previous life. That made things easier, and it shows that there are more human connections between our institutions than we are aware of." This human dimension, related to the fact that Brussels is a small capital, makes for stronger institutional connections, because people know and respect each other. "That makes it easier to have a successful conversation and to achieve results that are useful for the institutions involved."

Oana admits that NATO remains a very male-dominated environment. But with a feminist Secretary General, who has been openly sharing his views with fellow leaders, such as the Canadian Prime Minister, Justin Trudeau, there is a realisation that more needs to be done to bring about systemic change. Oana tries to play her part by mentoring colleagues, both male

you can't just have men in grey suits everywhere. We're past that

and female, and serving as a role model: "I am in favor of meritocracy, so I believe in hiring people on the basis of what they can do and how well they can do it. I would say it is the best way to promote both men and women. It is about having the right person for the job. But giving an opportunity to women to step up is, of course, what is sometimes missing." However, she does not seem convinced that a quota system works. Oana concludes: "Clearly, you can't just have men in grey suits everywhere. This does not work. We're past that." Oana favours a system that focuses on getting the best candidate for a job, yet also pays attention to giving women the chance to step up.

Wisdom, Tips, Dos & Don'ts for a Woman Leader-to-be

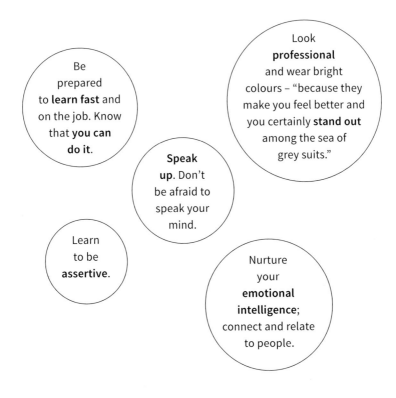

Be prepared to **learn fast** and on the job. Know that **you can do it.**

Look **professional** and wear bright colours – "because they make you feel better and you certainly **stand out** among the sea of grey suits."

Speak up. Don't be afraid to speak your mind.

Learn to be **assertive.**

Nurture your **emotional intelligence**; connect and relate to people.

Ann Mettler

German/Swedish. Head of the European Political Strategy Centre, European Commission. Self-made entrepreneur and thinker.

If You Do It, It Better Be Worth It

Success Comes from Doing what You Want to Do

There is a common thread throughout Ann Mettler's life: she does what she wants to do. With an air of determination, passion and confidence, she has made her way to the corner office for our interview.

Ann changed her university studies from business to political science because she realised she needed to be passionate about the things she did. "I knew that I would only be successful if I could do what I wanted to do, and even if I wasn't going to be successful, I still wanted to study what I wanted to study … Maybe I would end up somewhere as a glorified secretary, but I thought I am just going to do that rather than doing business and not enjoying it."

Despite her family's discouragement, Ann switched university courses, and subsequently went to the United States in the early 1990s as part of her master's studies in political science. Ann was determined to leave the small German town where she grew up during the long Chancellorship of Helmut Kohl (1983-1998) and to follow her dream. There were no professional role models anywhere in Ann's childhood: "Growing up, I had a lot of wonderful people around me, but none of them professional women … I never had a coach, I never went to (women's) networks, I just sort of did it."

I come from of a sort of matriarchy and so for me it has always been a given that women can have a strong presence

However, Ann credits her family background as a crucial factor in making her who she is today. She had a strong mother and four sisters – a rather atypical family environment. Ann never questioned that women could do anything. "I was raised by an extraordinary, wonderful mother and I am one of five girls. I come from of a sort of matriarchy and so for me it has always been a given that women can have a strong presence."

Studying in the US in the 1990s was a transformative experience. While there, Ann encountered many self-confident, successful professional women in academia. Ann likewise remarked on the women she met later while working in Switzerland: "When I worked at the World Economic Forum in Geneva, many of the women who worked there were French. They were smart, attractive women who had children and came back to work after three months' maternity leave. Women who were now mothers and professionals."

Young and Female – a Double Handicap?

After working at the World Economic Forum for three years where she last served as Director for Europe, Ann came to Brussels in 2003 and, together with her husband, co-founded the Lisbon Council, a think tank focusing on economic and social affairs in Europe. Despite having confidence in her own abilities and skills, Ann found that men frequently treated her differently to men, especially in the earlier years of her professional career. She cites a recurring pattern: "You are part of a debate and you make a suggestion or an intervention and no one pays attention. Then a man who is 20 years older says more or less exactly the same thing and everyone is like 'oh, that is so interesting and clever'." Ann notes that this frequently happens to women at the beginning of their career, when it can be difficult to be taken seriously by male counterparts or senior colleagues.

Ann made it her strategy to deal with these experiences by ignoring them and moving on – unless it was worth fighting for recognition: "If it is really something important to me, I will proactively try to take charge or take the floor. It really depends on the situation and how much I care about it." As Ann became more experienced she found that it got easier to be recognised; and, in the public policy arena, professional titles help and people generally assume that more experience makes you wiser.

Ann gives great credit to her husband whom she considers a feminist: "For him I am a complete equal". He has always been supportive of her professional moves and a partner in every sense of the word, especially indeed when they were also professional partners. In her current post at the European Commission as head of the in-house think tank, she misses the flexibility of her previous job, where she was self-employed, shared certain tasks with her husband and was frequently able to work from home. She saw her children more often and was there for special occasions. Yet work obligations were always present, as is often the case for self-employed people: "When you are self-employed, you're essentially always working."

Nowadays she has more job security and more predictable, albeit long, working hours. Once she leaves the office and is at home, she really is at home and focuses on the family. She believes this provides a better professional-personal life balance: "On weekends, I'll check in electronically at work once a day, but it's just different. Mentally it is different."

Having it All is Constant Improvisation

Ann's response to the famous question of Anne-Marie Slaughter, "Can women have it all?", is: "Yes, but it is difficult and not guaranteed. Various things need to fall into place such as a career trajectory and family planning

... and then if you can have a career and you do have children, comes the difficult part of how to combine all of that. ... It is constant improvisation."

Having been self-employed, "this ability to essentially make a living for yourself and create something out of nothing" is a source of pride for Ann. Building on that experience, she is also particularly grateful that in her

Can women have it all? Yes, but it is constant improvisation

new job at the European Commission she is able to run a think tank that creates space for creative, blue sky-thinking about public policy in Europe: "This is what I want my legacy to be: a space where people can come and really (think) outside the box. A space for unconventional ideas and people. I have an open mind and that's what I would like to create."

She attributes her professional success to being authentic and not being too accommodating about what people want or expect from her. She is proud to have created opportunities to go to places and organisations where she had more chances to evolve professionally and as a person: "Had I never left Germany, I honestly don't know what or who I would be today, but I 100% know I wouldn't be sitting here."

Leadership is About Management and Much More

While Ann admits that she has never thought much about her own leadership style, she has clear views on what makes a good leader. According to Ann, a good leader needs to be a good manager and be inspirational and motivating. "You need to motivate yourself and you need to be able to motivate others. But I would say the most important factor – by a long way – is being a good manager, and delivering on what you are supposed to deliver. And by the way, that is a huge opportunity for women." Ann sees women as generally better organised and better managers.

Ann describes her leadership style as a mixture of encouraging her staff and looking over their shoulders. She speaks of her own style as being questioning, inventive, constantly solution-oriented and "customer-centred". With experience and seniority, Ann says, her leadership qualities became second nature to her, just like her organisational skills: "I am a mixture of empowerment and micro-management in the sense that I like to empower (people) by letting them work independently but also find it very important to know what is going on in all teams … I am curious and questioning, I reject the notion that something is impossible. I improvise and innovate; it is the art of taking constraints and turning them into solutions and ideas."

A European in Brussels

Ann speaks of herself as having no national identity: "If I am anything, I am European." Brussels was a natural place for her to settle and establish herself. She sees Brussels as a place offering many opportunities but acknowledges that it is essential to be able to work well with many different people of different nationalities and cultures: "You can keep your national identity but you need to be very comfortable with anyone."

Ann also describes Brussels as a tough place. Having been a founder of an institution and an entrepreneur, Ann says: "I think Brussels is a place of opportunity but it is not a place that is naturally welcoming or friendly to people who come here to change things and shake things up. But if you are a talented professional, then you can do anything here." Motivated, keen professionals can make it in this city, according to Ann. Young people should not be discouraged by not always being taken seriously at the beginning.

> *Brussels is not a place that is naturally welcoming or friendly to people who come here to change things*

But what is still missing, according to Ann, is a critical mass of women in leadership positions, which is necessary for women's abilities and contributions to stop being questioned. Ann believes that the ability to speak publicly is crucial to advancing and creating a successful career. The city is a place of numerous events and meetings. "I have found it really important in Brussels to speak publicly, because if you can't convey whatever it is you are thinking in a compelling way, then it is hard to be heard and seen."

Ladies, don't be shy, apply! – **Reaching Gender Parity in a Large Institution**

As head of the European Commission's think tank, a post she has held since 2014, Ann can attest to the increasing awareness about the absence of women in decision-making positions in the EU institutions. Much of this is driven by President Juncker himself who gave Kristalina Georgieva, European Commissioner for Budget and Human Resources from 2014-2016, a mandate to raise the proportion of women in management positions to 40% by 2019. Georgieva herself served as a role model but also regularly convened meetings of women in senior posts (director level) for exchanges among peers.

This institutional awareness is a rather recent phenomenon, but ultimately it leads to old, male management teams being finally broken up. Women in senior positions, including Ann, are now able to encourage fellow female colleagues to apply for senior positions. Ann herself has been able to build a directorate with a large number of women: "I recently saw a chart showing women in the different Directorate-Generals (DGs) or departments and apparently we are one of the ones with the most women. It's natural for me (because) I don't think that way. I don't hire men or women, but qualified people."

A pipeline of talented female candidates needs to be created as it is fundamental to giving more recognition to women in mid-level career positions and enabling them to move up. And as Ann also notes, men have to be intellectually engaged in the goal of reaching gender parity. According to her, these two elements are the key to bringing about structural changes. Influenced by her past professional experience working on economics and economic policies, Ann stresses the importance of understanding the economic benefits of having more gender equality. But she would also like to see men mobilised through the experience of mixed teams. Ann is convinced that it will allow them to understand how it generates productive, cordial working environments and brings in diverse ideas and perspectives: "Essentially (it is) about being able to advance and for that it is not just a function of rules (but) it is a lot about traditions," Ann notes.

Ann Mettler – the person invited by President Juncker to bring innovative thinking to the European Commission – concludes that more gender parity is important, "but not because women are charity cases. We have a contribution to make and it is in everyone's interest to recognise that."

Wisdom, Tips, Dos & Don'ts for a Woman leader-to-be

Speak up and practise public speaking. Say what you have to say.

Be **authentic**!

Pay attention to your professional appearance. Wear colourful clothes so you **stand out**.

Have a job that is meaningful for you: "**If you do it**, it better be **worth it**"

Be **courageous** and develop your confidence.

Monique Pariat

French. Director General of European Civil Protection and Humanitarian Aid Operations (ECHO), European Commission. Overseeing the EU's global humanitarian assistance programmes, and on a smaller scale subtly creating space for working parents.

Go for It – You Can be a Driver of Change

The Quintessential European

Monique Pariat has been working at the European Commission for nearly 30 years. Since her early years, Europe has played an important role in Monique's life. She grew up in France, a founding member of the European Community. Growing up in the 1960s and 70s, Monique's German language teacher at secondary school encouraged her to join an exchange programme that would enable her to learn more about other parts of Europe. While studying at university in Strasbourg, Monique became an enthusiastic supporter of European integration, and of the EU project as a whole: "I had a very inspiring professor and I immediately fell in love with European law, European integration and the European construction."

She naturally went on to take a Master's degree at the College of Europe in Bruges, the European university known for teaching professionals who go on to have careers in European affairs. Monique is one of their success stories and is representative of the "European model career" for many people in Brussels.

Monique's career has been based at one of the core EU institutions, the European Commission (EC). But before joining the Commission, Monique worked on European affairs at the Association of European Chambers of Commerce and Industry and then in the representative office of the Italian Chambers of Commerce and Industry to the EU in Brussels.

As Monique worked her way up at the European Commission from Administrator to Director General, she dealt with a wide range of issues: industry, fisheries, education and culture, agriculture, justice and home affairs, civil protection and humanitarian aid operations. Monique is, however, one of the few Directors General who has never worked in a Commissioner's *cabinet*, or private office, which is usually a major stepping stone in "making it" professionally within the EU institutions. Monique explains that she succeeded in her career by excelling at what she does through working hard and being on top of her files, developing contacts and networks, and being well organised.

While Monique was inspired by the European project, she was also motivated by the examples of strong, independent, intelligent European women, such as Marie Curie, Benoîte Groult and Françoise Giroud – scientists, writers, journalists. Her mix of passion, inspiration by role models, and her mother's encouragement (to strive for financial independence) empowered Monique to pursue her career. At the EC, supervisors or colleagues continued to give Monique the confidence to excel and advance: "Support came often from my supervisors. People who believed in me gave me the confidence to get out of my comfort zone and move upwards."

Women Still Have a Larger Responsibility at Home

Monique rejects the idea she has been treated differently because she is a woman. However, she did feel treated differently when she became a mother: "The big difference nowadays is not so much being a man or a woman, it is having a family or not; having to find the right balance between your private life, family life and professional life. And that is the moment where I felt it became more complicated." Her German father-in-law expected her to stay home after Monique's first child was born: "He could not figure out that it was not for financial reasons that I wanted to continue working. Half joking he even offered part of his pension to keep me home!" Monique explains that some years later, her then boss refused her a promotion, based on the argument that she was still young and could wait. Since she was pregnant with her third child she took the opportunity to counter: "I might be too young for a promotion, but soon I will be too old for another child." His "congratulation answer" was to inform her about the existence of the pill!

> *The big difference nowadays is not so much being a man or a woman, it is having a family or not*

For Monique, women and men are both responsible for moving towards a life where home- and care-related tasks are shared equally. This can be attained with more self-awareness and by ensuring "mum's tasks" are shared between partners: "There is still this cultural responsibility that falls more on women's shoulders." But she recognises a change nowadays: "Younger men are more used to having a working wife and are used to sharing the tasks of family life. It is becoming more accepted at work, including increasingly by supervisors, that a man leaves work at 6 o'clock to pick up the kids from the crèche. We will reach our objective of equality in the workplace when the problem is no longer a woman's problem, but just a parent's problem."

Striking a balance between her private and professional life "required a lot of assertiveness. It also required self-confidence, pushing myself (to be able to say 'I have to go') and the capacity to stick to my limits. Family life never prevented me from working hard but it was very difficult because you couldn't expect your boss to tell you 'it is time for you to go home'." Now her children are grown up and Monique says: "I have absolutely no regrets because having a good work-life balance is very important." She had to be the driver for change at work to allow for this balance.

Monique does not like the question "Can women have it all?" According to Monique, nobody has it all. The question – for women and men – should not be about having it all, but about making choices according to their priorities and values: "We have to know what we want, what matters to us." And what matters for Monique is to have a successful professional career as well as having a family – i.e. driving the change to make it possible herself.

No Leader Has It All

According to Monique, a leader needs to have a determined attitude, robust common sense, and the wisdom to surround themselves with people with complementary competencies: "No one has it all in terms of skills, so good leaders surround themselves with the right mix of competences to complement his or her own."

Monique does not appreciate putting men and women in "stereotyped boxes". Having said this, she observes that male leaders can often be more power-driven, and female leaders less territorial and more collaborative. But there are counter-examples on both sides! Working in teams is what defines Monique's leadership style. She tries to keep a sense of humour, likes to boost her team members, and be tuned in to the requirements of the environment: "I work in a policy area where you face disasters and conflict situations that are really heavy-going, so if you didn't have a good, positive attitude you'd just go back to bed and cover yourself with the duvet!"

good leaders surround themselves with the right mix of competences

Monique admits that at the beginning of her career she was more impulsive and reactive. She gained confidence in her leadership style over the years, learnt to trust her intuition, and to use common sense. These days, when a difficult matter comes up, she takes time to reflect whenever possible: "There is no perfect solution; situations are relative to the environment in which they take place. Moreover, there are moments where if you are too involved in the problem you may not be able to find the best solution. So you need to 'get out of the ballroom to the balcony' (to see the situation from a different perspective). This is something I have learnt over the years: take some distance, sleep on it, look at it fresh the next day, and come to a better decision."

Brussels – a European City

Monique's Brussels is the Brussels of the European institutions: powerful, multicultural, with a dual nature – the capital of a small country and the heart of a powerful international actor. A city where there is a constant striving for compromise. "We are often in the driving seat for something that will be legally binding, so decision-making requires the capacity to move around different cultural approaches, different ways of reacting, different approaches to a problem and also the necessity to find compromise and joint solutions."

When Monique joined the European Commission, the EU was composed of only twelve member states. It now has 28 members (which will fall to 27 after Brexit), so Monique has experienced the EU's constant evolution and restructurings from within: "What was very rewarding for me was the way we integrated people from different backgrounds. Very rapidly we found it natural to work with each other – at the beginning with the Spanish, then with the Finns and then with the Czechs and the Romanians." The cultural and national diversity makes professionals in Brussels realise that you cannot speak the same way to different nationalities.

Monique thinks of the different European peoples as a big family and of Brussels as a place where "everybody can feel both at home and not far away from home". Monique refers to the rather unique "Brussels expat identity", a mix of multiple layers of nationalities (multiple languages, mixed couples, mixed families, mixed social networks). This identity has both advantages and disadvantages. On the positive side, Brussels expats are more exposed to and used to co-existing with other cultures; they speak multiple languages on a daily basis and their children grow up in multi-national environments. On the down side, it is easy to lose the sense of where people truly belong – they no longer fit their national identities, which frequently become too narrow for their enlarged horizons.

Expatriates in Brussels share the experience of living abroad, feeling European, yet not feeling Belgian or feeling completely at home. As an example, Monique speaks of her own children, born with a multiple identity: "My children consider themselves as French and German but their home is Brussels, not so much France or Germany, and they feel closer to people who have a similar international background. They just feel European: my son, who plays for a US university soccer team, when asked which flag should be raised for him replied: 'the European Flag'!"

A Europe for Women …

To Monique, Brussels offers many opportunities for women, even if it can still remain challenging at times. She recalls a dinner in the 1990s which she attended, as a spouse, with her husband at the residence of the Swiss ambassador. During the evening, it automatically happened that two conversational groups formed – one of the men, the other of the women. The other women were appalled to find out that Monique was a working mother, who wanted to work. Nowadays, things have changed.

… But Not Just for Women

Structural changes need to happen for both working mothers and fathers and the family as a whole and therefore should not been claimed as a benefit for women solely. She believes that if couples put the problem in terms of sharing responsibilities (at work/at home), it will be easier to get men on board: "A child has usually two parents, so they both have to be involved."

Good practices in the process of promoting women to senior positions have to become the norm and it helps to have more women in senior management positions to ensure more professional women get recruited at all levels. Mentoring relationships, networks among women within the European Commission, equal opportunity days where women can share their experiences, have all contributed greatly to paving the way for more women to apply and obtain management posts. And, according to Monique: "You also have a growing number of men in the Commission that are convinced that working in a mixed environment is an asset."

Mentoring relationships, networks among women … have all contributed greatly

Equal opportunities policies require a modern management culture and strategic work organisation. This includes a clear division of tasks, independent work methods, and systems of back-ups and deputies. Moreover, Monique stresses the importance of balanced working hours. "I try to organise meetings with a structured agenda, a limited time frame and within working hours. I try to be respectful of those who have to leave. I ensure a good back-up system so that I can always have a continuity of operations. This makes colleagues more comfortable to leave if they know there is someone else who can take over and more motivated to accept some flexibility when needed. Finally an extended but disciplined use of remote modern technologies also contributes to a better balance of professional and family responsibilities."

Wisdom, Tips, Dos & Don'ts for a Woman Leader-to-be

Sleep on difficult issues: **make decisions fresh** the next day.

Share family responsibilities with your partner.

Don't fall for **stereotypes**: Go for what motivates you!

Be clear about your values, make **choices** based upon your **values**, and be prepared to adjust your values and your choices. Be ready to **change your mind**.

Consider different perspectives on a matter: **move from ballroom to balcony** when needed.

Françoise Pissart

Belgian. Managing Director at the King Baudouin Foundation.
One of the few women leaders in the philanthropy sector.

Learn from Your Failures and then Move On

A Lack of Role Models

Françoise Pissart, Director at the King Baudouin Foundation (KBF) for the last 15 years, is a well-prepared, assertive and candid woman. Françoise discovered feminism in Canada during her Masters studies in sociology. Having returned to Brussels to start her career, Françoise was acutely aware of the lack of women to mentor and inspire her. There were not enough role models to help encourage the careers of young women. And at the time, the philanthropic world was dominated by men in the top positions.

Given the absence of female role models and mentors, Françoise gives a lot of credit to her long-time boss, Luc Tayart de Borms, Managing Director at the King Baudouin Foundation, for supporting her: "Luc really believed that I would be able to work as a leader and he empowered me in a perfect way: supporting, encouraging, putting me forward, giving me responsibilities." Françoise has had no female boss who really empowered her during her career and she misses the experience of female solidarity at work.

After taking up her first leadership position, Françoise soon decided to take a coach to help her further develop her skills. Coaching gave her the consistent support she needed, from developing general management skills in her first position, to her current position as Director at KBF, where she is in charge of a significant part of the Foundation's budget. Leading a complex structure, having authority over men and women, some of them older than her, and handling all the intricacies of this new role was challenging at the beginning. Holding such responsibilities required considerable effort and resilience, and obliged Françoise to constantly learn, to leave her comfort zone and to develop strategies to overcome her difficulties.

Handling Everyday Sexism

When Françoise became one of KBF's four Directors in 1999, the Foundation's Board of Trustees was mainly composed of men – men more senior than her and with long careers behind them. This was not an easy situation for Françoise: "I was about 40 and I had that feeling that they were just looking at me as a little girl." Even today, after over 15 years at KBF, Françoise is sometimes still at the receiving end of patronising behaviour by men.

Over the years, Françoise has refined her strategies to handle the situations where she faces gender stereotypes and related challenges. She deliberately chooses to address these with a good mix of self-awareness, humour, empathy – and authority. Françoise explains that her response depends on the gravity of the situation, but her general rule is to refrain from impulsive and emotional reactions. Usually, after some time, she does a self-assessment *à froid*: "I evaluate what happened in the situation and then I analyse if what I did was wrong. If I made a mistake, I will do my best to improve.

Like everybody, I do not have all the skills and I am continuing to work on improving where necessary." If Françoise concludes that the root cause of the problem was bias, she will define the best approach to address the problem: either with her superiors or directly with those involved in the situation. Ultimately, she concludes, it is about developing effective coping strategies to deal with gender discrimination: "You need strategies to face this kind of situation. You need to know how you will react."

You need strategies to face this kind of situation. You need to know how you will react

Knowing Oneself and the Image One Portrays

Over the course of her professional career, one particular experience contributed to Françoise's self-awareness and allowed her to advance and consciously grow in her leadership style. During a leadership training session, Françoise was taken aback by the feedback she received from other participants. They had the impression that she always wanted to be perfect, that she was very clear and very well organised. While this was appreciated, they said they could not feel the human side of her leadership. Françoise knew that the person her training colleagues were describing was not the real Françoise. Nevertheless, she was grateful to discover that there was a clear discrepancy between who she felt she was and the image she projected. This realisation, Françoise recalls, "was really good news for me because I then decided that my leadership would be more natural, closer to myself, attuned to my personality. This means showing more enthusiasm, more spontaneity, being friendlier with people … After this, my leadership became more effective and I enjoyed my role more. So it was really an important moment for me to understand how I was coming across and what I needed to do to address this perception."

Learning by Doing… and by Failing

Françoise admits that learning that she came across as a cold perfectionist was not an easy insight – but a very important one. Françoise points out the pattern of women's perfectionism: "In a lot of cases affecting many women, there is a familiar pattern. You were very good during your studies, then you began to work, then your boss sees that you are very good, and he promotes you. You have to lead people and you think you still have to be perfect. However, that is impossible because being a leader is being able to adapt to different kinds of situations and to anticipate things that go wrong. And you cannot learn to adapt if you don't experience these situations." This reasoning led her to understand the importance of failure: "You learn if you fail, so it is very important not to focus obsessively on your failures, but to use them to learn and to move on."

Françoise recommends: "Ask for feedback from people you trust. Sometimes, if you have a good relationship with colleagues, whatever their position, ask them what

Ask for feedback from people you trust ... you will learn a lot

they think about the way you are doing things, and then you will learn a lot and can adapt." Françoise has consciously refined her leadership style and is determined to continue improving it. Among other elements, Françoise considers participation and inclusion to be important elements of her leadership. She strives to develop participatory processes, fosters and appeals to the creativity of colleagues, and actively listens to other people's ideas before making a decision. However, Françoise also underlines the importance of being clear that, at the end of the consultation process, it is the boss who decides.

Work-Family Balance is One of My Biggest Accomplishments

To achieve a balance between her family and professional life, Françoise believes that she has made conscious sacrifices in terms of her social life, leisure, cultural activities or sports. But this is not something she regrets – on the contrary, she feels very proud of her personal-professional balance. Françoise is convinced that women (and men) can have it all – when "it all" means everything that matters to them.

Maintaining the right balance between work and family life was crucial to Françoise from early in her career. This turned out to be a big challenge, especially during the 4 years she lived and worked in Brussels with her three young children while her husband worked and lived in The Hague. Despite the challenges of this experience, Françoise concludes enthusiastically: "Of course we can have everything. I'm not saying that it's easy, especially if you have young children, but it's not impossible." To illustrate how Françoise juggled these competing demands, she shares a recent personal anecdote:

"I had been invited to take part in a debate on women in leadership. So the day before, over dinner, I asked my children: 'What has been the most difficult thing for you about having your mother working full-time?' I didn't say anything else, just waited. They just looked at me and said 'what are you talking about?'!"

Françoise has advice about choosing the right partner: "When you fall in love, it is not usually your first thought to think about whether your partner will do everything in the kitchen, look after the baby and do all those (domestic) things. You choose your partner using other criteria. But try to make a good choice, build your life with somebody who at the minimum is open to applying equality between men and women in the private sphere." She also decided to keep things simple – such as not living far from the office, finding schools for the children that are not at the opposite side of town and keeping their after-school activities close to home. According to Françoise, by concentrating your life in one limited geographical area, "you will also be able to benefit from solidarity with neighbours and other parents". Simplifying life also means, whenever possible, paying someone to help at home: "Even when I was working for an NGO and my husband didn't earn a big salary, we always paid for a cleaner to help us at home", she says, adding that being flexible and, indeed, asking for and being given flexibility at work was critical.

Crucial Ingredients to Being a Good Leader

While "we have to adapt our leadership to the situation and the people we are working with", Françoise identifies some key qualities that a good leader needs to have: they should be optimistic when it comes to dealing with difficulties and obstacles; they should be courageous and enjoy challenges; and they must be able to connect with people and build a vision. She believes that a good leader needs to be a team player, good at managing people, willing to listen, generous with individual support and able to foster solidarity among colleagues.

On Male and Female Leadership Styles: We Do not Lead in the Same Way

Françoise states: "I don't think we lead in one way. What influences your style of leadership most is your personality, regardless of whether you are a man or woman." Having said that, Françoise still observes a difference in attitudes that she relates to socio-cultural causes: "In a mixed group of my generation, my experience is that men don't want to lose face. Especially those who have some responsibilities and who are very convinced that they are the right man in the right place." Furthermore, "for me, as a woman, what matters, at the end of a meeting, is if the decision is good." However, even after over a decade of experience and whilst in a leadership position, sometimes "I still have the impression that I'm really in a competition (with male interlocutors in meetings)."

my experience is that men don't want to lose face

For Françoise, the most important message to those men in "gatekeeping positions" is to show them they can profit from having a gender-diverse team in terms of productivity and innovative ideas.

Brussels: Crossing the Local, National and European Levels

Françoise looks on Brussels as a very political city where people constantly strive to influence the decision-making process. Therefore, she considers the most important skills for a leader in Brussels are the ability to manage different stakeholders, awareness of the EU's particular institutional ways of working, and the ability to connect the different institutional levels. Working effectively at the European level was something that Françoise learned step-by-step. For her, the hardest challenge when working at that level has been finding a common agenda and turning the difficulties (in understanding each other) into a strength. This is very difficult at the start, considering the variety of different stakeholders in Brussels. But once you know how it works, you can use this knowledge effectively: "The first time you go to a conference, you don't know anybody. When you go to the fifth one, you know one-third or half of the room. In the end, it's a small world."

Nonetheless, to be successful in Brussels, Françoise says that "you have to accept that you won't know everything and everybody". You need to be able to find your way with a certain amount of uncertainty. Being a leader in Brussels also means being able to take decisions even if you do not have all the information. She argues that it is important to take risks and accept that "I don't know everything, I don't know everybody, but I have the right colleague(s) and the King Baudouin Foundation has the right partner organisations to do the work. I'm confident that we are achieving good results together."

Women are More Likely to Leave their Brussels Career

While Brussels offers a multitude of great opportunities to both young women and men, Françoise observes that women frequently leave their jobs to follow their husbands back to their home countries or third country destinations, especially if they decide to have children. "I saw too many young women leaving Brussels, leaving their jobs to go back home, to follow their partners. They had a beautiful career in front of them, but they felt it would have been too difficult." She encourages young women to resist and embrace the challenges ahead. Françoise did not follow her husband when he took a different job in The Netherlands. Being economically dependent on someone else and sacrificing her career was not an option for Françoise. Françoise encourages new arrivals in Brussels to become "part of the city as a whole", and to get involved in networking as a way of creating "solidarity networks" within their communities of work, their neighbourhoods and their national groupings.

Too Few Women in Decision-Making in the Philanthropy Sector in Europe

Only a few women have made it to decision-making positions in the philanthropy sector. This also applies to the governing boards of philanthropic institutions. Françoise acknowledges, however, the progress that her own foundation has made in this respect: "We do have a balanced board, which was not the case 20 years ago."

Foundations often work on local and societal issues, and for that reason, Françoise stresses the importance of developing more sensitivity and awareness of gender equality. This is essential to have a real impact on the ground and to develop gender mainstreaming in general. She and KBF are part of a gender initiative to promote a gender lens to the work of foundations throughout Europe – created a few years ago, together with the European Foundation Centre (EFC), an umbrella organisation for European foundations. However, due to differences between the participating foundations' missions, structures, countries of origin, and organisational cultures, developing a common agenda within this gender group has not been easy. Yet, for Françoise, fostering dialogue and exchange is essential to raise awareness, and learning from other sectors will eventually have an impact on the philanthropic sector.

It is Always Possible to Find Very Able and Enthusiastic Women

Good practices for promoting women in leadership positions include having quotas. "Nobody likes that, but I think it's the only way to progress," Françoise observes. "When you are looking for women (for a position or a conference), the first reaction is to say there are no women. But of course, there may be not many women who are well-known, because their priority is to be active, not necessarily to become well-known. With a little bit of effort and creative searching, it's always possible to find very competent and enthusiastic women." These women should be supported to become more visible and engaged, to apply more frequently for open positions – even if they think they don't fulfil each and every one of the recruitment criteria. Managers should promote this culture of inclusion, and hiring managers should be particularly proactive in looking for the strongest candidates, which may mean looking to other new and non-traditional sources and networks.

Concretely, Françoise also suggests a number of changes to be implemented. These include flexible working hours, meetings held only during business hours, and transparency and accountability in hiring, promotion and firing decisions, among others.

Her own organisation, KBF, did a recent analysis of the composition of their juries and selection committees – they include over 2000 individuals who assist KBF in reviewing proposals – with the objectives of raising awareness and developing greater diversity of thinking. According to Françoise, the findings were "… awful. Even if there is a nice gender balance in the general composition of those advisory groups, we have twice as many male as female chairs. So we immediately decided to share those roles more equally." A review of their contracts with civil society grantees revealed that the majority of the people signing the contracts were men, but the person doing the work was still a woman. This is not particularly surprising, given that senior roles in civil society, as elsewhere, are disproportionately held by men. Nevertheless, these examples of good practice and awareness-raising are ensuring that gender inequalities cannot be swept under the carpet anymore.

Wisdom, Tips, Dos & Don'ts for Women Leaders-to-be

Be **confident**. If you are promoted, it means that you are the **right person**. Do not doubt that.

Take time to deal with complex matters. Whenever possible, **sleep on it** and then respond.

Do not stay in the shadows; **be visible** in what you do.

Your team has to feel that they can **take risks** and fail, too. It allows you and your team to grow and develop.

Allow yourself to fail, so you can **learn** from your mistakes.

Be **bold** and ask for **feedback** on how you are doing – to learn and get better.

Helga Schmid

German. Secretary General of the European External Action Service. Elegant, emphatic, a relationship builder and negotiator in a male-dominated setting: international relations.

Gender Diversity is Not about Women: It is about Equal Opportunities

A Life Shaped by Europe's History

Helga's formative years were shaped by Germany's history. Interested in history and politics and intrigued by the Franco-German reconciliation efforts after the Second World War, Helga went to Paris after high school graduation to teach German and take classes at the Sorbonne. Coming from a southern German, Catholic and conservative background, this immersion in a different culture and society was an "eye-opener", Helga recalls. "I discovered that it was actually fun to work in a foreign country. Not to be surrounded just by Germans, but to work abroad in a foreign language." This is when Helga discovered that she wanted to continue working in an international context and "also to promote Germany's image abroad". She joined the Foreign Service as one of nine women among the 60 trainees in her year group.

While Helga was at a Russian language training in London in the late 1980s, the Berlin Wall fell – another defining moment for her: "I belong to the generation of Germans who didn't believe that the wall would ever come down. Never, ever." The wall (which divided Berlin from 1961-1989) had symbolised the separation of Eastern and Western countries in Europe during the Cold War. Its fall paved the way for German reunification (1990) and further enlargement of the European Union. Helga recalls that historic moment in her life and the world's history: "I had a little flat in the centre of London, which was owned by an Anglican pastor. I came back from my class and he said that the Berlin wall is open, and I said 'you must be kidding'. The whole world was celebrating, and I will always remember the headlines the day after. It was a miracle."

Helga worked in various positions in the German Ministry of European Affairs and Foreign Ministry. Under German Foreign Minister Joschka Fischer, Helga advanced to being Deputy Head of Office and then to Head of Political Staff and Office, at a time when Germany was militarily engaged in the Balkans as well as in Afghanistan. Helga was sent to Brussels in 2006 to work for Javier Solana, who had the roles of Secretary General of the Council of the European Union and High Representative for the Common Foreign and Security Policy. There she led the Policy Planning and Early Warning Unit. With the entry into force of the Lisbon Treaty, Helga switched to the European External Action Service (EEAS) where she became Deputy Secretary General for Political Affairs. There, she has worked under the leadership of Lady Catherine Ashton and then Federica Mogherini, High Representatives of the Union for Foreign Affairs and Security Policy.

Throughout Helga's formative years, her father played an especially instrumental role: "It was definitely my father who pushed me to go for it and not accept any obstacles. He was very proud of me and he still is, even at the age of 91 years. So in my early years his support was probably quite important." Helga also describes herself as lucky for having been able to work in a *cabinet* for two Deputy Foreign Ministers at a very early stage in her career, which opened up the way to her first posting abroad in Washington DC: "I would have never had the chance if Irmgard Schwaetzer and Ursula Seiler-Albring, then Deputy Foreign Ministers, had not promoted me. This was a very good example of women promoting women."

Judgement and Inequity

Helga has numerous stories of being treated differently because she was a woman. Especially when she was young, there were cases of "well-meaning" men who recommended that she find a husband rather than a diplomatic post, when she was taking the entrance exam for the Foreign Service. Helga also became acquainted with the role of the media and male peers in uncritically accepting, replicating and promoting centuries-old gender stereotypes: women were judged by beauty and looks and their brains and abilities put to the side. "That puts a lot of pressure on you! I really felt that I had to prove my abilities", Helga acknowledges. It was also a significant step for her to realise that in order to gain recognition, she had to move out of "soft" portfolios, such as culture, and gain experience in the so-called "hard" subject areas, such as disarmament and security. Helga is convinced that "knowing their stuff" and being assertive helps women early on to succeed, as it did for her, even when it is hard to have the courage to take action in hostile contexts.

in order to gain recognition, she had to move out of "soft" portfolios

Today, her senior role gives her authority and she rarely faces discriminatory situations. For example, her gender was not an issue during negotiations, to which the EU was a party, over Iran's nuclear programme. "Federica Mogherini, myself, and on occasion an almost all-female team on the EU's side dealt with an all-male team on the Iranian side. The Iranians were very professional, so I never felt that gender was a disadvantage." Despite this, Helga recollects other moments in international negotiations where she has experienced male peers, more used to dealing with other men, not paying attention. On these occasions, she finds her best strategy is to be assertive and have the courage to impose herself, even if that is not the "nice" attitude that most women normally like to display. Another recent development is that today there are more women in management and senior management, so women are no longer alone all the time in male-only environments: "That explains why my ambition as Secretary General is to make sure that we have an increased percentage of women in management positions."

A Balancing Act

Helga admits that balancing a professional career with a personal life is difficult, and that there are structural issues still preventing equal opportunities for men and women: "Anne-Marie Slaughter really has a point in highlighting these difficulties. I don't have kids, but I have many female friends who are really struggling to combine everything, even though we are in the 21st century." She criticises the fact that women are still seen as the primary carers for children and that not enough is done to encourage or enable men who want to do more, such as taking paternity leave. Further, Helga argues that it is essential to create working environments that allow both mothers and fathers to have a better family-career balance as well as being able to balance two careers.

Balancing the Need to Listen with the Need to Be Assertive

Helga's commitment and passion for her work is evident. She is a woman whose assertiveness and a certain stubbornness got her to where she is today, a position where she can make important changes in the world.

For Helga, a good leader is someone who is willing to take risks for a cause. She respects German Chancellor Angela Merkel for her stance on migration, following the mass influx of refugees into Europe in the summer of 2015: "She is someone who takes risks, but also someone who is considerate and takes decisions based on facts and evidence."

While she is hesitant to follow stereotypes and make generalisations, she does see distinct female leadership qualities. According to Helga, women listen more, engage, know their facts well, and are better negotiators than men: "Women have the ability to understand better where the other side is coming from. They can show empathy and through that, they manage to gradually bring their counterparts to their side and find consensus. Sometimes you just need to listen first, to understand what your interlocutor's interest is. Then, you can try to reconcile the different needs at the table."

She describes her own style as empathetic but also assertive at times, whenever the situation requires it. It is very important to her to build personal relationships. Helga has a tremendous network of contacts in

Investing in networks costs a lot of time but in the end it pays off

which she has invested throughout the years: "It is not only the professional exchange, it is about the personal relationships. This is something I learned when I did my diplomatic training. Investing in networks costs a lot of time but in the end it pays off, and it allows you to really connect with people in a different way."

Her own leadership style has changed, she concedes. At the beginning, Helga was somewhat shy, risk-averse and low-key. She rapidly learnt that in order to pursue her objectives, she had to assert herself, be visible and make sure others knew she was good: "I learnt to promote myself." And she learnt this from male peers! Early in her career, when she was working for the then German Foreign Minister Klaus Kinkel, Helga was informed by the female secretaries of the *cabinet* that her male colleagues were meeting without her. "When there would be such a meeting, I just went, knocked, entered and then said 'Sorry, I missed the note to meet', which I really hated saying because it felt demeaning – but it worked."

When Helga arrived in Brussels in 2006 she quickly realised that she needed to establish networks. In contrast to Germany, where the hierarchies of the ministries dictate the modus operandi, in Brussels a particular position is not enough to get your voice heard: "You really have to establish your network and find your way around. If being a good networker is a quality, you definitely need it in Brussels". This is a very complex working environment, as Helga concedes. Relationships and networks are therefore crucial to success.

Moreover, Helga describes Brussels as an environment where one needs to focus on consensus-building, unlike countries which have fewer stakeholders to be taken into account, such as the US. "This need to find compromises is quite unique, but it is also our strength. You have to forge consensus – but this does not mean you have to undermine your own interests. It is a way of moving forward." Evidently, this quality is sometimes perceived as a weakness by non-EU interlocutors and other stakeholders, so Helga acknowledges that "we constantly need to explain and show that we are delivering. That is the best way to show that we are a successful model."

Empowering Women: Walking the Talk

When Helga first arrived in Brussels there were only a few women's networks. There was much to be done, so Helga decided to set up a network of women inside the European External Action Service. This led to Helga sometimes facing the suspicion of men who felt disadvantaged and excluded, but she reassured them that these initiatives are not against them: "It is about equal opportunities". Helga is determined to create more favourable working conditions that allow both women and men to work on their careers, take parental leave or have the opportunity to follow their spouses abroad and not be disadvantaged in their own professional advancement.

Replicating the model of her first bosses and mentors, Helga's day-to-day work in the EEAS involves mainstreaming gender equality and women's empowerment. Externally, she always tries to ensure that women sit at the negotiating table, women's rights are taken into consideration in peace agreements, and gender is taken into account in preparing the agenda for summits or evaluations. "I always put these issues on the agenda. In my experience, there is always lip service paid. Sometimes men have the tendency to say 'yeah, women's empowerment. Yeah, fine, box ticked, let's move on'. But I urge us to discuss it, what does it mean, how do we implement this?" Sometimes, the results can be frustrating and this is where resilience is crucial.

Internally, aside from her EEAS women's network, Helga mentors, gives advice and frequently hosts women who have advanced in international relations and diplomatic services to speak to the EEAS staff, both men and women alike. As Secretary General she would like to see the implementation of the 40% target of women in senior positions set by former Commissioner Georgieva for the European Commission.

The responsibility for changing things cannot be just down to Helga and the EEAS gender advisor. It requires a wider group – of both men and women – to ensure that gender equality is always on the agenda and is acted upon. While Helga knows that it is necessary to start from a high executive level to push the issue, she remains frustrated about how difficult it is to put mechanisms in place. "Everyone knows that agreements are most sustainable when women are involved in the negotiations. But what I deplore is that there is still not enough support to bring more women to the negotiating tables and into decision-making in general." For her, this is also about keeping and

Everyone knows that agreements are most sustainable when women are involved

restoring the EU's positive image in its external relations, especially when engaging with third countries: "In Africa, Asia, wherever the EU has a positive image despite the crisis, we need to talk more about who we are and what we do."

Wisdom, Tips, Dos & Don'ts for a Woman Leader-to-be

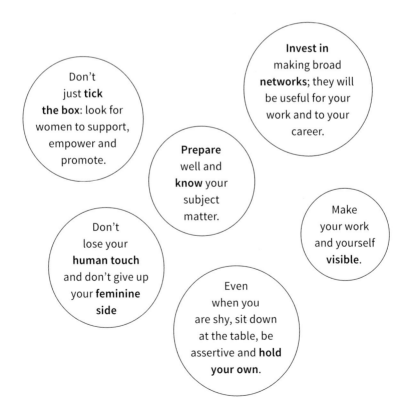

Don't just **tick the box**: look for women to support, empower and promote.

Invest in making broad **networks**; they will be useful for your work and to your career.

Prepare well and **know** your subject matter.

Don't lose your **human touch** and don't give up your **feminine side**

Make your work and yourself **visible**.

Even when you are shy, sit down at the table, be assertive and **hold your own**.

Shéhérazade Semsar-de Boisséson

French/Iranian. Managing Director of POLITICO. Family-oriented entrepreneur at the intersection of media and business.

Women Who Seek to be Equal to Men Lack Ambition

The Nonconformist

Shéhérazade does not identify herself as a feminist. She does not agree much with "this gender equality stuff". She does not like what she describes as "labels" or "simplistic boxes", and rejects the type of narrative of gender equality that posits that men and women should think, behave and feel in the same way. Shéhérazade strongly defends the freedom to be unique and the need to escape globalised "standardisation trends". "I just don't believe we're all the same, as much as the big tech companies and the media want us all to be the same."

Shéhérazade comes across as charismatic, pragmatic and entrepreneurial. She came to Brussels from Paris in 2013 when she purchased European Voice, which she later sold to POLITICO, following which she became the first managing director of POLITICO's European operation. She handles all business aspects of this large media outlet that serves the Brussels European affairs communities.

From Iran to a Global Career

Throughout her life and career, family has played a major role for Shéhérazade. She explains that there were three particularly significant periods in her life: the Iranian revolution in 1979, her university studies in the US, and setting up her first company at the age of 23 in France.

Uncompromising, practical and daring, she describes herself as a European with an "Oriental" perspective on certain things, such as the importance of family and education. She talks passionately about her Iranian matriarchal heritage and culture, and her role model is undoubtedly her mother, whom she describes as an inspiring, "very entrepreneurial and hands-on" person. When Ayatollah Khomeini overthrew the Shah of the Pahlavi dynasty, Shéhérazade's father, journalist Mehdi Semsar, was thrown into in prison. At the time when the Islamic Revolutionary Court staged daily trials and executions, it was Shéhérazade's mother who kept delaying his execution through appeals and calls: "When my father was in prison, what she had to do was make sure he was not on the list to be executed".

Shéhérazade's mother had to make sure he was not on the list to be executed

Her mother organised the family's departure from Iran, when Shéhérazade was only 10 years old. Shéhérazade later chose Georgetown University in Washington DC to do her undergraduate studies and earn a Master's degree in International Finance. It was here that Shéhérazade met the woman who became a role model for her: Madeleine Albright, the first female US

Secretary of State (1997–2001). The latter had experienced exile herself, originally from the former Czechoslovakia: "Albright has an amazing success story, and she is just an amazing person. In her leadership role, in her political role and as a professor."

When she returned to France after her studies, Shéhérazade started her own company at the age of 23, the Development Institute International (DII), which became one of France's leading conference providers. In 2013, after she acquired the European Voice newspaper from the Economist Group, she re-launched its website and created new services. In December 2014, POLITICO and Axel Springer acquired European Voice and DII. It was at POLITICO that Shéhérazade became, for the first time, part of a larger executive team with several male peers. "I've never had to go through or live through gender discrimination in this corporate world where there is a lot of tension between men and women." This is her first piece of advice to other women: "Start your own company" – *be independent*.

Gender discrimination in the workplace was not a major problem for Shéhérazade and she believes men are generally becoming aware of their need to promote more women to leading positions. Nonetheless, she has witnessed sexist situations, especially in meetings, and has reacted strongly to protect other women. Shéhérazade developed a coping strategy to deal with situations when men wanted to meet her at what she refers to as absurd hours, such as during family dinner time: "I just told them 'well, the problem is that as I don't have a wife, I'm going to go home and we will find a proper time to meet'. They would usually take 5 minutes to understand the joke … So yes, I can be a little bit obnoxious, but that is because I owned my companies, which made it probably easier as I had the freedom and confidence."

Family and Children are the Big Rocks in Life

Several years before joining POLITICO, Shéhérazade had other investors who wanted to buy one of the companies she owned. They told her: "Your company could have made so much more revenue and grown several international offices." Her reply was simple: "I know all that. But I built a family simultaneously."

Shéhérazade concedes that there were staff at home helping to take care of the children. But she and her husband made sure that they never travelled simultaneously for work, and grandparents from both sides were always present. It is very clear that her priority is her family and especially her children: "my biggest accomplishment is my family, and then it is the companies I built. I would not have liked it to be the other way around." When answering what "having it all" means for her, she responds: "What is all? Is it being a senior partner at McKinsey or at JP Morgan and working 18 hours a day and having a family? I don't know if that is all, but I don't believe those two are compatible for anyone. And I don't wish that for my daughters."

So how did Shéhérazade manage to put her family first and still develop several successful companies? Knowing her own priorities and developing effective time management skills were two key elements. The tough part was not only developing the rigorous discipline required but also accepting that one person simply "can't do it all" in today's demanding, fast-paced and aggressive society: "You know there are things you just have to say 'no' to, and be relaxed about."

The other winning strategy for Shéhérazade was to never look on her professional life as a constraint. She loves doing what she does: "I don't mind working on vacation. I once told my son that work is my hobby. Because the second you consider work as a constraint, you start making a very big division in your life." Nonetheless, Shéhérazade sticks to a structured routine in her daily 12-hour working day: "I have breakfast with the kids. I always get to work early, so they get up early. I always go home for dinner – my rule is that I have to be home by six o'clock. I've been very strict about that. I have dinner with them. And then I start work again around nine-thirty or ten. That's something I've seen as absolutely non-negotiable if you want to build a family and have a successful career."

Women and Men are Different

She wonders whether it is due to her Oriental background, as she puts it, that she has always thought of men and women having different roles, but Shéhérazade is unconvinced about that part of the "equality" debate that expects that that men and women should think, behave and feel in the same way: "We have different needs. Biologically we are different, as much as there is a societal pressure to impose an illusion that we are the same. We operate differently." This is the underlying reasoning behind Shéhérazade's scepticism in relation to the gender equality debates. "I don't believe in equality as understood in this way. I keep on telling my daughter, don't be like a man. I don't think husbands can be wives and boys don't have to be like girls. We're not all the same. We all have our very own special identity, our sex and origin is part of that unique identity. I just feel that we're trying to making individuals become a standardised, gender free, digital consumer with no true individual identity."

We're not all the same ... our sex and origin is part of that unique identity

Shéhérazade believes there are specific issues that need to be tackled: the gender education gap, women's right to protected motherhood, the social pressure against women who decide to be "just mothers", etc. She remains confident but cautious: "I believe in time. I think the more women are being educated, the more they are going to be on boards. I do think in Europe and in the US women are getting up there. They are highly educated." However, a career is not enough for Shéhérazade: "Will today's girls be able to have a happy family life, will they be able to bring up the kids with values? I think that is going to be a tougher challenge".

Brussels and the Major Challenges of the Day

According to Shéhérazade, for a business leader operating in Brussels, a predominantly political city, it is important to be able to understand the trends: political, economic, technological, and so on. Leaders need to be able to adapt to a challenging, and constantly changing, environment. Being a leader these days is extremely complex: "You have a lot of variables to work with. You have the variable of employees being happy, the shareholders being happy, figuring out how you're not going to be disrupted, and figuring out how you can disrupt the others, figuring out how to pay all the social costs..." Brussels' regulatory bodies need to have vision, says Shéhérazade, and be able to join forces with the business sector: "There are six big issues in the world that we have to deal with – artificial intelligence, digitisation, healthcare, feeding the world, climate change, water scarcity – and Washington and Brussels have to be able to deal with these issues for the Western world. That really is the core of Brussels – it's how much the private sector is part of the solution, and how much the policy-makers are part of the solution." These big challenges make leadership very complex today, and require a very unique set of skills, both in the private and public sector: understanding and leading through constant change, following trends and global dynamics, anticipating and knowing how to deal with these. She concludes by saying Brussels is a multidisciplinary place: "It's a city where you need history, politics, international affairs and human relations to get your message through."

Today's Business World is in Constant Competition

There is ruthless competitiveness in today's globalised world. Shéhérazade acknowledges that it is hard for CEOs and managers to keep their businesses performing in today's world. In this aggressive context, politically incorrect thoughts might emerge: "We have to pay out salaries every week. So how do you reconcile individual needs and corporate needs? It's not obvious. The competition is also coming from companies based in countries where employees' rights and protection are simply non-existent. Maternity leave has financial consequences for the company, that's a reality. So we can't blame the 'corporate men' either, because they're running companies and have to ensure efficiency and sustainability in the long term for as many as possible." What does this mean for women – and men – today, who wish to reconcile careers and family? According to Shéhérazade, for small businesses it can actually be easier: "In small organisations you can actually handle it quite well, because when you have great employees – men or women, with or without kids – you can let them take time off; there is less of a 'career battle' to be won internally."

Good Leadership is Leading by Example. End of story!

Shéhérazade declares: "Who's the best leader for me? Jesus. Jesus did what he said. He washed his disciples' feet to show the example. That is true leadership: humility, doing what you say and saying what you do." Shéhérazade tries to lead by example. Throughout her career, she has noticed that women tend to take more responsibility than men, and hence also admit mistakes and search for solutions more candidly and rapidly.

While she says that women are probably better at execution of tasks than at leadership, she also acknowledges that "women are great leaders, because as mothers they always lead naturally by example. We have a value system with which we were brought up, and with which we are bringing up our kids, which gives us a very strong set of guiding principles." For Shéhérazade, men have a public tradition of being more visionary leaders than women, even if things are changing: "The world has become so connected that you just can't run things the old way, in the very patriarchal top-down way." "Leadership has changed and I don't think it's linked only to women. It's linked to the whole environment, the interconnection of stakeholders, the interconnection of employees, the interconnection of personal-professional life."

Today a leader needs to make sure that his or her team knows why they work, their purpose, what they are working towards. Shéhérazade says: "I see a lot of companies coming back to the *why*." For her, this represents a paradigm shift: "For many years we have tried to create economic well-being, and then at some stage we achieved it. We have it all: security, economic stability, family, jobs. But we're lacking the meaning and the sense of purpose."

*We have it all.
But we're lacking
the meaning and the
sense of purpose*

Women Should Engage in Politics and in Creating Enterprises

Shéhérazade does not fully support quotas – "yes, women are part of society, so they have to be part of decision-making, but this should come naturally". She describes herself as more demanding of women than of men: "I think nothing's worse than having incompetent women. I know there may be a lot of incompetent men. But that's not a reason to have incompetent women." For her, the way forward is for women to be more involved in public policy and to run businesses. Of course, this should never be done without continuing to value their roles as family-builders. For Shéhérazade, women running small and medium enterprises, more education for women and having more women in peace negotiations is much more important than having women on boards. This is one of the reasons why Shéhérazade continues to support the University of Georgetown, where she serves currently on its Board of Directors and was involved in the establishment of the Georgetown Institute for Women, Peace and Security under the leadership of Melanne Verveer.

Wisdom, Tips, Dos & Don'ts for a Leader-to-be

Don't over-stress when it comes to bringing career and family together: **you'll make it!**

Don't do anything you **don't want** to do.

Lead others as you want to be **led**.

Be **independent**: start your own business.

When you have an opportunity to **build a family**, do it. And **never** sacrifice it for your professional life.

Pastora Valero

Spanish. Vice President at CISCO Systems. One of the first Southern European women to reach such a top position in her company. Technology is her great ally in balancing work and four children.

When Men Share Responsibilities, Gender Equality Will Happen

A Curious Mind

Pastora left her hometown in the south of Spain, Seville, just after having graduated in law. She was a curious 21-year-old and wanted to get international experience, learn foreign languages and discover the world outside her country. She specifically wanted to understand what the

European Union was all about – Spain had just joined in 1986, together with Portugal, in the third wave of EU enlargement while Pastora was at university.

Pastora came to Brussels and started her career as an anti-dumping and trade lawyer in a Belgian law firm. She was not very familiar with anti-dumping law, but had decided to take the leap: "I said 'I'm going to do it'. They interviewed me and they offered me an opportunity, and I just did it." She could not have known then how this decision would be a watershed in her life: "I always thought I'd go back to Spain at some point: 'I'm just going to do some EU law, gain some EU kind of practice, then I'm going to go back'. And then I never went back!" After just a few weeks in Brussels, she was sent to Mexico to deal with an anti-dumping case. However, her career "was not about a key moment but some defining moments – making different moves, and not always taking the easiest route. Above all taking risks – and not being afraid of making mistakes." Pastora eventually joined Cisco Systems in 2003, after receiving an offer from the European Commission. In deciding between the two offers, she considered that "one was more stable (the Commission), the other was more of a risk." Pastora's inquisitive personality was drawn to the cosmopolitan, dynamic environment of an American company, where she could learn from different people: "I chose Cisco and have never regretted it."

Support from All Sides

Pastora comes from a large family and was born at the end of the Francoist era, the autocratic regime which lasted for four decades from the late 1930s. Her mother worked. With three university degrees (history, journalism and media), her mother was a journalist and TV presenter, a city councillor and a university professor. Pastora's mother was her biggest inspiration and role model. "My mum always had a professional career. She never made any distinctions at home between girls and boys, and always encouraged me to pursue my dreams, to study, have a career and my own economic independence."

My mum always encouraged me to pursue my dreams

Pastora's husband plays an equally important role in her life. Pastora considers a supportive husband key to having a professional career.

"A husband that views your career as important as his and who, rather than making you feel guilty when you are not there, is there when you cannot be, is important." They discussed careers and family at an early stage of their relationship. In addition, Pastora calls herself lucky for having always had supportive bosses, especially those bringing a diverse approach to executive leadership: a focus on collaboration, an innovative vision and who believe in leading by example when it comes to the importance of increasing gender diversity at the executive leadership level.

Unconscious Bias and Subtle Inequalities

Don't allow anyone – including yourself – to place limits on what you are capable of delivering

At the current stage of her career, Pastora says that she no longer experiences gender discrimination. However, on looking back, she has met and observed "micro-inequities" – gestures which often go unnoticed, like getting repeatedly interrupted in meetings or not having your points taken seriously. Pastora thinks that at the start of her career she lacked assertiveness. Indeed, as a general rule, she finds that women do not put themselves forward enough, with the result that they often fail to contribute to group discussions effectively or lead decisively. Pastora herself worked on her self-awareness and self-confidence in order to be able to handle these situations. "In the end the most powerful tool you have to combat these attitudes is yourself. Don't allow anyone – including yourself – to place limits on what you believe you are capable of delivering."

Technology – a Blessing in our Pursuit of Having it All?

With four children Pastora is convinced that men and women can have it all. The question is rather how people define the balance between their professional and personal lives. For Pastora this means that she will be 100% with her job sometimes, and at other times 100% with the family. She highlights that this is "her solution" and that each choice comes with the need to make some sacrifices: "there's no right or wrong answer."

Pastora puts no rigid spatial boundaries between the office and the home. In this way, she can have dinner with her family and then work from her home desk at night after the children go to bed. Her work is about results, not office presence, and today's technology gives her the ability to succeed in this way. Pastora appreciates CISCO's flexibility in enabling her to adjust her working hours to be with her family and contribute to the success of a company that works in multiple time zones. Technology has been key for her, but she still believes "companies need to do a better job to allow for the career-family balance – and to make sure women don't need to opt out when they become mothers." That means that workplaces should allow women to slow down at particular periods in their careers instead of "punishing" them for taking time off from work to look after their family.

Despite the big help of technology in organising her life and giving her flexibility to combine work and family, Pastora still has to make choices. In this sense, Pastora believes that balancing family and a career can only work with support: "I do have household help and a supporting infrastructure at home, and this is particularly important when children are young and you cannot always be physically there for them."

Leading Collective Accomplishments

Besides her family, Pastora is proud to have a job that she is passionate about. She has built a supportive team, comprised of colleagues who complement her skills and allow her to continue to learn. She believes in enabling people to grow and shine, and is proud when someone makes progress under her leadership. Pastora stresses the importance of surrounding yourself with people who know more than you and who can one day surpass you. For her, this is courageous leadership at work.

Pastora is also part of various initiatives that allow her to inspire, coach and facilitate women's professional advancement. "I hope one day to be able to say that I inspired other women or that I helped other women succeed. If there is a way to make it easier for women to climb up the ladder and I can contribute to that, I would be very happy."

Leadership is as Much about the Leader as it is about the Team

For Pastora, today's society requires different leadership approaches and capabilities than in the past. Nowadays, the capacity to build personal interactions matters more than projecting authority, for instance. Defining features of good leadership for Pastora are authenticity, collaboration, ambition and the ability to lead by example. Equally important is allowing one's team to excel. This means leaders needs to build their own self-confidence.

women have unique capabilities that actually play to our advantage in today's world

Pastora argues that the qualities that make a good leader do not vary between men and women. It is the person that determines the quality of leadership. Still, Pastora believes women have an edge on some leadership traits over men: "I do think women have unique capabilities that actually play to our advantage in today's world. Women leaders tend to be more collaborative, cooperative, they listen more and build bridges." She frequently observes women being empathetic.

Pastora likes to think of herself as practising an inclusive leadership style, where she fosters collaboration and knowledge-sharing across the team. She admits to still struggling at times to balance the need to delegate with the wish to check details and be hands-on. "While I really try to empower the teams to be autonomous, there are times when I need to get engaged in the particulars. Finding that right – often elusive – balance is key to keeping up the motivation."

Brussels – an Ally to Women

Pastora finds many of the leadership skills that are often attributed to women to be useful in the Brussels context. For example, the complexity of the EU decision-making set-up requires negotiating skills and the ability to build consensus. It requires resilience and patience. This skills-set is sometimes difficult to explain to American counterparts, she chuckles, who ponder why certain negotiation processes take "so long" in Europe.

Creating Diversity in the Corporate Sector

Pastora describes the business sector as a mixed bag in terms of promoting the professional advancement of women. She refers to a 2016 World Economic Forum report on women and work that states that across industries, women currently make up on average 33% of junior level staff, 24% of mid-level staff, 15% of senior level staff and 9% of CEOs. Companies are just starting to get more interested in the question of where women go between the 33% and 15%.

Pastora's own technology industry is developing multiple initiatives to make women role models more visible, creating new programmes to inspire the next generation and motivate middle-managers to remain in the pipeline. Pastora says: "My area of work – lobbying and policy – is much more gender balanced than engineering." She is happy to observe that more men around her are sharing family responsibilities: "They are also learning and changing. It's great to see a man saying he can't do a conference call at 6pm, because he has to pick up the kids." It is another step to change the working culture more generally.

While she sees several examples of good practices already emerging, Pastora would like to see more efforts towards gender-inclusive methodologies and working cultures. Specific benchmarks and concrete measures are needed: these include ensuring gender diversity in interviewing panels, among pre-selected candidates and amongst selected candidates; setting clear diversity targets and operating in full transparency and accountability; "opt-out" and "opt-in" clauses to allow women and men to take time off from work for family-related reasons at certain times and afterwards rejoin the workforce; provision and take up of childcare facilities and paternity leave; and data on women's recruitment and promotions.

Pastora concludes by arguing that it is essential to involve male colleagues in achieving greater gender diversity on all levels of a company, especially CEOs and managers: "They are key to set the tone and make diversity an authentic and constant feature of the way an organisation operates. Women need to be at the table and men need to be engaged in the conversations. When men share responsibilities, gender equality is going to happen."

Wisdom, Tips, Dos & Don'ts for a Woman Leader-to-be

Can women have it all? There's **no right or wrong** answer.

You are the **only person** who should be managing your career and defining what you can achieve.

Work on your consensus building skills but know when to **stick to your guns**.

Have the **confidence** to surround yourself with people as talented as yourself. The trick is in bringing this talent together and **making a difference**.

Know when to **delegate** and when to get into details.

Margot Wallström

Swedish. Minister for Foreign Affairs. A politician since a young age, she is the mastermind of the first feminist foreign policy.

Nothing about Women without Women

A Woman Entering Politics

It is personal relationships that have shaped Margot Wallström, her personality and the progression of her career as a political leader. Family and friends provided a secure and nurturing environment and encouraged Margot to stand up for what she believed and become an activist, community leader and politician. While she was still at school, a neighbour encouraged Margot to get involved in politics and organise around relevant local demands such as better public transportation to town, community space for young people, etc. Margot did so, and her career took off. At the age of 25 Margot became a member of the Swedish Parliament; at 34 she became Deputy Minister of Civil Affairs (Consumer Affairs, Women, Church and Youth). In the following years she also held the positions of Minister for Culture and Minister for Social Affairs.

Margot grew up and developed her political conscience during the social-democratic government of Prime Minister Olof Palme. A pivotal and charismatic politician in Sweden, Palme was considered by some both domestically and internationally as a polarising figure, especially regarding his non-alignment policy towards the superpowers and his support for numerous "Third World" liberation movements. Palme inspired Margot and she recalls a speech when he was the Social Democratic party leader: "I remember the way he described what you can do as an ordinary individual, to understand the society you live in and what kind of power that gives you. That was a life-changing speech for me."

Margot did not set out to be a frontrunner. Her passion and interest in civic affairs, her determined beliefs enabled her personal experience as politician. One of her latest successes is the adoption of a new feminist foreign policy strategy for Sweden, in 2014. "Countries of the EU must lead by example. To be credible, we need to show that there is a link between our internal and external action and that we apply a gender perspective when we build our organisations, form our negotiating teams and staff our missions."

Gender Bias, Even in Sweden

In spite of the well-known Scandinavian "open mentality", gender-biased treatment is not unfamiliar to Margot. She experienced it as a young Member of Parliament when both her youth and her gender seemed to disqualify her in the eyes of older male colleagues from being a serious counterpart. Margot experienced similar treatment later, during her tenure at the European Commission. "Whilst with the European Commission, my *chef du cabinet* was a man. When delegations came to visit me, as Commissioner, they would turn to him and would address him. It was not very wise from their side to do that", Margot chuckles. Margot normally ignored this kind of behaviour, though she noticed it every time. However, she would at times gently ask all male delegations: "Are there no women in your business?" She noticed that frequently her counterparts were oblivious and did not understand the question. She felt that individual gender awareness was very much linked to how far ahead the respective state was in terms of women's advancement and diversity matters, which was not far in the 1990s – even in Sweden.

Family and Work: Use Every Day of Your Parental Leave!

In the 1980s, Sweden was a country whose welfare state was among the world's most generous. Margot considers this social protection, like tax reforms and childcare, essential for women to participate in public life and still have a family. Independently of her professional positions, she consistently took full advantage of that: "I used every single day of my parental leave."

Despite the advancement of family support and childcare in her country, Margot and her husband found that balancing professional and personal life was difficult. She and her husband took turns, made choices, juggled responsibilities: "You cannot have it all. You just have to realise that at some point you have to work a little less to be able to be more with the kids. And then you can go back, when you are older and you can work more. I don't think anybody should believe that you can have it all. You hopefully can share with a good partner and you have to adapt".

Throughout her life, Margot has always had the firm belief that her children come first. When her kids were small, Margot was a Member of Parliament. To be able to spend time with her family, she would go home early and work after the children were in bed. Nevertheless, like

I don't think anybody should believe that you can have it all

many working mothers, she went through moments of guilt: "There will always be times when you have a really bad conscience because you have to go to work and work a lot." The fact that she was working for a better society and her sons were very proud of her made this easier to deal with: "You have to make them proud of what you do". So, even if combining family and career was challenging, Margot has no regrets: "You also have to be proud of the choices you make."

In fact, Margot does not hesitate to say that she sees her biggest accomplishment in her two sons. Professionally, she cherishes having had the opportunity to put her heart into matters that she cares about, to go for something important, meaningful. In the pursuit of her career, Margot aspired to be authentic, to be true to herself as well as to be kind to others. Being able to plan well and have fun – to enjoy one's job – are essential to being successful in one's professional endeavours. For women and men alike.

Knowing Yourself – Self-Awareness as a Key to Leadership

Having held leadership positions for more than 30 years, Margot considers self-awareness the first quality of a good leader: "Know yourself. Know your strengths and shortcomings, as a person and as a leader". Listening, engaging, giving responsibilities, being friendly and knowing the people you work with are additional important qualities that help in the exercise of leadership.

Know yourself. Know your strengths and shortcomings, as a person and as a leader

Margot acknowledges different styles of leadership for men and women and attributes them to differences in experience and knowledge: "I think women leaders, when they come in, shape new methods to exercise leadership and that's good." Margot hesitates to generalise, but ends up saying that women develop leadership skills beyond strict rational approaches: "How much is genetic and how much is stemming from our different life experiences? I do not know." What she does know is that she very often sees women looking at each other in meetings and saying wordlessly to each other: "We would not do it that way."

Margot comes back to the importance of self-awareness when describing her own style of leading. Leadership, as she says, "brings out the best and the worst in us. You are under such heavy pressure that you will sometimes excel. And, at times, you will be totally tired, frustrated and mad, sad or just grumpy, and not very nice. This happens to all of us. You just have to accept that you have those sides and be aware of them."

To compensate for this reality, Margot recommends surrounding yourself with supportive, critical and complementary people. In her own case, Margot's staff and colleagues need to know what situations she can handle well and adapt consequently. They sometimes also need to compensate for her imperfections: "They have to know that I am impatient and I do not have an eye for details. I need people who can do the details." In conclusion, self-awareness and team-work also go with modesty, and Margot warns against the risks of big egos: "Don't think leadership is a God-given thing. These days you can fall very hard and very far."

Brussels – an Elitist Town

Margot's take on Brussels has been shaped both by her years as a resident and her frequent visits to Brussels. She lived in the city for 10 years when she was Commissioner for the Environment and then Commissioner and Vice President for Institutional Relations and Communication Strategy. Since 2014, she has returned frequently to Brussels as Foreign Minister and representative of Sweden in the Foreign Affairs Council and other meetings. Margot regards Brussels as a unique place.

However, Margot considers Brussels' European spheres to be elitist: "Many people – especially those who come to work in or around the European institutions – are well-educated, well-paid, they are really well-off. So it's easy, it's an easy life, in one way." But while Brussels offers an easy life in some ways, it is also extremely stressful and competitive, with many hierarchies and highly structured European institutions, which are often difficult to navigate for newcomers. These difficulties are real, especially for professional women in middle management who encounter the greatest hurdles in climbing up the ladder. Rather than speaking about a glass ceiling in Brussels, Margot uses a term coined by Laura Liswood, founder of the Council of Women World Leaders: "It is not a glass ceiling, it is a thick layer of men".

Women in Politics

Margot describes the practice of promoting women to senior decision-making positions in Europe as "unfinished business". Talking to us in 2016, with only three women among the 28 European Union foreign ministers, the situation remained "bad", with "strikingly few women".

Besides her extensive contributions to conceptualising the Swedish feminist foreign policy and influencing the EU agenda on these matters, Margot is also proactive in increasing gender equality in her own immediate professional circle. She has started an informal network of women foreign ministers. Its purpose is creating awareness, fostering bonds among the few women in foreign minister positions, and exchanging information, experiences and best practices on how to overcome gender barriers.

Sometimes simply the threat of introducing quotas is enough to change the reality on the ground

At the EU level, she applauds the work that former Commissioner Georgieva has done to increase the proportion of women in senior positions in the European Commission. Margot is an unequivocal advocate of quotas as a tool to promote women: "We know that we need a critical mass, at least 30% women, before we have a chance to influence and change for the better. Therefore, we ought to use this instrument (quotas) more. Sometimes simply the threat of introducing quotas is enough to change the reality on the ground … Gender equality is the unfinished business of our time and this must shape everything we do."

Wisdom, Tips, Dos & Don'ts for a Woman leader-to-be

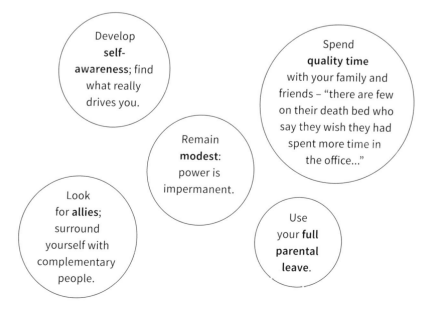

Develop **self-awareness**; find what really drives you.

Spend **quality time** with your family and friends – "there are few on their death bed who say they wish they had spent more time in the office…"

Remain **modest**: power is impermanent.

Look for **allies**; surround yourself with complementary people.

Use your **full parental leave**.

PART III

REFLECTIONS AND CONCLUSIONS

Tips from the Top: How Remarkable Women Lead in Brussels

10 Takeaways from the Stories

The 14 women we interviewed have very diverse histories, are of different nationalities and cultural backgrounds, and exhibit different leadership styles. Their diversity shows us that there are many different ways in which you can be a leader. At the same time, there are also some striking commonalities in their stories which we want to highlight in this chapter.

1. Leadership is a Continuous Learning Process

If you want to be a leader, you need to be aware that you are entering a life-long learning process. By viewing your professional career as a work in progress and allowing yourself to evolve with authenticity, you will gradually develop a personal style that suits both you and the changing needs of your work and professional context.

Many of our interviewees agreed that leadership does not "just happen" and that it is never a "finished product". Most of them experienced their career evolution in a rather gradual manner, taking risks, wrestling for and gaining new responsibilities, surmounting challenges.

Having said this, it was very interesting to hear that you can be a leader without really thinking it through as an outcome. Several interviewees said they "just" want to do their work and if they lead as part of that, that is great for them – i.e. gaining power and a formal position was not part of their initial purpose but it sort of "happened to them" as a result of what they wanted to accomplish.

Given that we focused on women living in Brussels, most of our interviewees have had important experiences away from their home countries that triggered their career path. Overall, our interviewees were all clear that while becoming a leader is not easy, the sacrifices are worth it because there is a sense of gratification and accomplishment.

2. Grab all the Encouragement and Support You Can Get – and Then Pass It On!

Receiving support and encouragement early in life was crucial for all our interviewees. It helped them to gain self-confidence and to make choices. For many of them, this support and encouragement was provided through the family, parents in particular, who were role models or simply believed in them and were sources of encouragement. For others, it was networks of friends or professional contacts – individuals who served as mentors (formally or informally), advisors at school or university, who gave inspiration, guidance and advice that encouraged them to progress.

The majority of our interviewees who have children stressed the importance of having a true partnership with the person you share your life with. This resonates strongly with Sheryl Sandberg's point about making your partner a real partner in her famous book "Lean In: Women, Work and the Will to Lead" (2013). Couples who act as a team and share the stimuli of two careers, as well as the family project, with all its trials and all its blessings, seem to be a winning model. The role of the spouse or partner who does his or her share at home with the children was considered fundamental, a sine qua non to attain a balance between career and a family life – even to the point where some referred to it as the most important "career decision" that a woman could ever make. The advice was nicely encapsulated in the phrase: "Don't marry a dinosaur!"

Couples who act as a team seem to be a winning model

But it also means that women should ease up on being perfectionists, including at home and, for instance, accept how their partner (imperfectly) does things at home. They must also be prepared to call on other types of help (housekeepers, nannies, au-pairs, babysitters) when that is feasible. As one woman commented: "We (women) have to consider that sometimes the daddies can also do the job." This partnership model of the "couple" with stable private lives can truly work in the long run, as both people in the relationship are empowered in their projects and talents, and co-create a family project that fits the needs and aspirations of both.

Finally, giving back, passing on one's own experience and advice made many of our interviewees speak about the need for women to help other women. This could be through mentoring or encouragement, or simply instilling certain principles and values about gender in one's own daughters (and sons).

3. Ingredients for Leadership Success

For our interviewees, good leaders are those who are able to bring about positive change in their organisations, among their staff and in their societies. In general, all agreed that a leader needs to lead by example, to demonstrate courage, vision, integrity, resilience, and the capacity to take unpopular decisions in the interest of organisational sustainability. "You cannot be liked by everybody" – which is particularly difficult for some women who may have been socialised from an early age to be pleasant, kind and lovable – was repeatedly mentioned.

to accept failure and learn from it were elements of the journey

Each of our interviewees had a different "recipe for success". However, these recipes share some ingredients: the capacity to work hard, to take risks; the courage to knock on closed doors, to accept new challenges, to create and/or choose unconventional solutions, and to overcome self-destructive beliefs, personal doubts and insecurity. Furthermore, many showed the ability for self-reflection: to accept failure and learn from it were elements of the journey that took the women we interviewed to where they are today.

With experience, these women became more daring. Several interviewees said they are ready to take more risks now than when they were younger. Maturity also seems to bring a renewed freedom in terms of assuming "femininity": several interviewees said they valued their "soft talents" (empathy, social skills, creativity) more now than at the beginning of their careers and they feel happier and more powerful that way.

4. Strive for Excellence not Perfection

All the women we interviewed repeatedly emphasised that it was important for women to excel in what they do. This means working hard and efficiently, being well prepared for meetings or briefings. But the point is to not just work well but *to be seen* to work well. In part, this chimes with the prevalent bias that women need to prove their worth more than men. But it is also about just being very good at what you do.

Remaining authentic, focusing on goals and continuing to believe that "with hard work everything is possible" is the mantra of many of these women.

Moreover, when women excel, they can more easily deflate attempts to patronise them or treat them with disdain. Still, many of our interviewees remarked that it has required a thick skin and resilience to deal with some of the belittling experiences throughout their careers, as well as the capacity to assess these situations case by case and decide on the best way of reacting.

At the same time, it is important to understand that nourishing excellence does not mean falling into the trap of perfectionism, of "being a superwoman", which can create a cycle of endless dissatisfaction with yourself. The "always know more than the others in the room" syndrome, as one of our interviewees mentioned, can too easily lead to pressure that becomes a recipe for lack of self-confidence, unsustainable workloads and expectations, stress, and consequential failure.

And finally, it is important to emphasise that excellence also draws on others. To give credit for one's entire team and make them shine is an essential part of leadership.

5. Be Serious about Tackling Discrimination

Most of the stories in this book confirm that gender-based discrimination is still alive. All of the interviewees had experienced or observed examples of women being treated differently from men in a negative way in professional situations. There were big and small inequities: situations where you know you are being treated differently from male peers, where you are excluded from a meeting, cut off in conversations, left out of social occasions catering only to men – all subtle incidents and invisible to those who do not experience it personally.

But there are also the more obvious contexts where clearly sexist remarks are made, such as the boss who tells his female employee when she informs him that she is pregnant: "You know there are birth control pills?", or the man who asks a woman who is applying for a job: "How are you going to do this job with a child at home?" While none of our interviewees had experienced extreme forms of sexual harassment, they had certainly heard about it.

As a few of our interviewees pointed out, motherhood is the ultimate test for gender equality in the workplace. Prejudice became more evident when the

motherhood is the ultimate test for gender equality in the workplace

interviewees returned to work as mothers. Most interviewees consider current organisational policies and culture largely inadequate when it comes to supporting, retaining and promoting female talent through the family-building phase that can last several years.

Gender-based discrimination, our interviewees agreed, decreases with age, experience and seniority. With formal power comes an authority that is difficult to disregard, even in situations where gender bias could normally exist and manifest itself. Yet many of our interviewees believe that a woman still needs to prove herself more, do more and better work, and demonstrate she is more qualified and experienced than her male peers to get to higher positions.

When faced with biased circumstances, the reactions and coping strategies of the interviewees varied. In some cases they let such incidents pass, though perhaps making a joke to create awareness, while preserving a professional manner. In other cases, they assertively call out men (or women) on their bias. What is important is to understand that speaking out against a bias is not "complaining" but about setting limits and illustrating what many people can still not see. When speaking up is not enough to solve the problem, it is important to seek institutional or external help and make use of tools such as "zero tolerance to sexual harassment" policies where they exist.

6. "Having it All" is about Individual Choice

There is no one-formula-fits-all to attain a balanced life and to achieve the "all" that makes one's life enjoyable and meaningful. There is, however, space for personal decisions and trade-offs, and each person needs to be aware of what is a priority (and what is not!) for them in the different phases of life.

Reactions to the "having it all" question inspired by Anne-Marie Slaughter's well known article "Why Women Still Can't Have it All" (The Atlantic, 2015), varied. Some interviewees dismissed the concept as simplistic and damaging as "it is an unattainable goal" (a myth), while others stressed that "yes, it is possible – if you plan, prioritise, share with your partner".

For most of the interviewees, what was important is the ability to define what "all" means for each individual person: "All" should be read as "all that matters to you" and not an "absolute all", and is therefore about individual choice and freedom. Opinions and individual strategies are very different and personal, as comes out from the different stories. Some are about time management and a couple's team work, others involve external support, IT support or even carefully planning birth and professional objectives in a life plan with "curves" that allow a mix of "career time" and "family time".

In the end, "having it all" is more about finding the strategy that works best for each person, defining the trade-offs that make sense to each different person, and reassessing them at every step of the way. Interestingly, in none of our interviews did anyone admit to any loss they may have experienced in going for their careers. While some talked in round-about ways about their sacrifices, thinking regretfully did not – perhaps surprisingly – feature in what they said.

7. Go Beyond the Male / Female Leadership Divide

The women interviewed rejected over-simplistic generalisations about gender-based differences between leaders: women and men are not two separate homogenous groups and there is as much diversity within the genders as across gender. What matters most in leadership is the sum of different elements: individual personality; the ability to overcome "traditional gender boxes" and combine conventional "male" and "female" attributes; and the skills that allow one to be versatile and aware of the particular cultural, social and professional context. It means being authentic, bringing the whole person to work. It means being self-confident without being arrogant; determined while collaborative; empathetic while assertive; inclusive while able to step up and take tough decisions; emotionally intelligent and self-regulated; consensual while results-oriented; and having the ability to take risks while preserving long-term sustainability.

It means being self-confident without being arrogant; determined while collaborative; empathetic while assertive ...

Many of the interviewees said that long-accepted gender differences are less pronounced in the younger generations of professionals they encounter. They said that young people have more freedom to choose; education, new gender models and legislation are giving more options, all leading to small steps in overcoming stereotypes. As a result, the interviewees acknowledged, they frequently work with younger women who are competitive, determined and self-confident, and with younger men who are collaborative and value time with their families.

8. Good Practices: Making a Difference

All the interviewees agreed that individual efforts accomplish little by themselves: what is key to achieving gender parity and real inclusion is systemic change, such as a supportive environment, networks, alliances, structural support provisions, and gender-sensitive regulations and policies at the level of the state as well as the employer. However, again, there are no "quick fixes" nor "one size fits all" approaches: each strategy needs to be tailor-made to the reality and needs of the person and/or the organisation and sector at stake.

Most interviewees agree that quotas are a necessary step to bring about real change, because "what gets measured gets done". Interestingly, most of the women mentioned that their opinion about quotas had changed over time: when younger, they believed they "didn't need quotas", that their talents and skill would allow them a fair career progression. With time, most of the interviewees realised that equal opportunities and "meritocracy" are not yet in place: women still have fewer opportunities and more invisible barriers than men. They need to prove their worth more and are subjected to harsher scrutiny when in leadership positions. As mothers, they frequently face professional and societal pressure.

It is the famous double bind: if a woman behaves in a "feminine" way, she is liked, but not respected or seen as a leader. If she operates in a "masculine" way, however, she is judged and disliked. For all these reasons, quotas as a means to ensure that there are more women available to compete for higher level positions can be important because they open a space, require a system to pay attention to talented women operating within its structures, demand the development of strategies, plans and monitoring.

For change to happen, a combination of these "hard measures" – quotas, targets, hard data, performance indicators, transparent and gender-conscious hiring and promotion practices – and "softer" strategies such as gender diversity programmes, training, mentoring, coaching, or accepting opt-in/opt-out or "ramp on/ramp off" options, are required to unveil gender bias and gradually change the mentalities of both men and women, as well as employers and employees. And aspiring to influence, being visible and having strong networks are all important in Brussels.

9. The "Other Half": Work with Men as Allies

All the women we interviewed consider it fundamental to involve men in the process of creating gender diversity in leadership. In general, they think that men are becoming more knowledgeable about the importance of gender diversity, especially younger and middle-aged men. Several interviewees observed that men are also taking on different roles for themselves (as professionals, as partners, fathers) and making choices that would have been eccentric in previous decades (e.g. taking paternity leave or sabbatical periods to spend time with family, leaving work early to spend time with the children, putting their career on hold – or simply slowing it down – to support their partners).

Engaging men, according to the interviewees, means starting with the men around you – staff, peers, bosses, family members – and making them understand what women face in their daily context as well as what they, as men, gain from more diversity and inclusion. This process of involving men also contributes to awareness of gender blind-spots – for instance, that they might unintentionally be speaking with women in a patronising manner, that they sometimes decide on the basis of discriminatory prejudice, old fashioned stereotypes and bias, or simply that they do not talk enough with the women around them about their realities at work.

10. Brussels Leadership Styles

Europe, and hence Brussels, signifies diversity in every respect. That is probably its biggest strength as well as its biggest challenge.

All the interviewees agreed that the city is a unique hub of power, situated in a truly international context with dynamics that are distinctive from other European capitals. It is an atypical locus of power – hosting the European Union project – and demands particular characteristics from leaders and managers that reflect European regional and cultural diversity. The terms Brussels, Europe and the EU are often used interchangeably, with little attention to their often multiple meanings. Many use "Brussels" to mean "Europe" and it points to the significance and magnitude of the all-encompassing European spirit that makes the capital of the EU a unique city.

there are distinctive features of what could be called a "Brussels/European leadership style"

Based on the interviews, it seems that there are distinctive features of what could be called a "Brussels/European leadership style", especially when compared with others, such as North-American leadership styles. "European features" include multicultural awareness, consensual negotiation techniques, process-centred negotiations, win-win solutions and emotional intelligence to reach cross-cultural and cross-sectorial agreements. In comparison to this, the perception of several interviewees is that, for example, while North Americans tend to be more forceful and results-oriented in their negotiation styles, more willing to take chances and make mistakes, Europeans are more policy- and process-oriented and therefore more dependent on negotiation and subtlety. Some mentioned that in the US, intimidation can be accepted as a respectable professional technique, while the collaborative style can be perceived as a weakness. In Brussels, it is the opposite.

Leaders in the politically charged Brussels environment are normally expected to be able to read complex situations; to understand the challenges of the numerous and often disconnected possibilities; to dissect multiple cultural codes and their political nuances; to persuade opponents, build allies and gain support from an inclusive base. In this context, there is more than ever a need for emotional intelligence. Leaders need to be visionary, perceptive, resilient, flexible, adaptable and prudent – yet gently prodding for change.

While this particular environment offers opportunities to any person – woman or man – who is a professional with a strong skill set and the capacity to network, the interviewees also conceded that the city is a tough place. It remains white male dominated, somewhat conservative, organised in silos, bureaucratic, elitist and very competitive – similar to other global power hubs. Awareness of the need for inclusion and the difficulties and relative absence of people with disabilities or ethnic minorities is only slowly emerging. Brussels remains a very exclusive place, with divergent European cultural standards about gender roles, many "old boy" networks and traditional gatekeepers. Female representation in different decision-making instances is not yet strong enough to create the necessary critical mass to create a more inclusive and diverse professional environment.

Brussels remains a very exclusive place, with many "old boy" networks

Moving Forward

This chapter contains our concluding reflections based on our professional experience, what we have learnt in the process of writing this book, and the many conversations we have had with numerous inspirational people working in Brussels, as well as in the areas of women's leadership and gender diversity.

1. The Power of Role Models

We are convinced that it is essential to make more visible the work of "pioneer" women – and men – if we want mentalities, behaviours and systems to evolve towards more justice, true equality or, at the very least, increased diversity. Role models are beneficial for stimulating open-minded new generations of leaders and to inspire all those willing to work towards creating inclusive cultures and values.

The profiles of the 14 interviewees make clear that there is no single way in which women can and do lead – just as there is no single way in which men lead. Restricting women to (old and new) boxes with pre-determined roles and skills is nothing but reinforcing stereotypical models again.

The profiles are clear: there are multiple ways to lead and leaders are the result of many identities; gender is certainly one identity, but also individual background, culture, class, personal choices, etc., play important and sometimes determining roles in shaping who a person is and how that person leads.

2. We Are All Pioneers

In today's complex world, gender roles can no longer be perceived as uniform. The speed of change in perceptions and attitudes towards gender is far from linear and differs from region to region, from country to country, from one professional sector to another, and from culture to culture. On the one hand, we are witnessing an increase in debates questioning traditional gender roles, recognising the importance of gender parity, and making visible the talented women who emerge across different professional sectors. On the other hand, we are observing reverse trends, expressed both in subtle and blatant ways. Recent examples of the latter are the bigoted remarks made by a Member of the European Parliament who finds it "normal" that women receive less pay than men "because they are weaker, they are smaller, and they are less intelligent" (Euronews, 2017); the bragging of US President Donald Trump about his sexual assaults on women during his campaign; or the legislative changes being made that worsen women's rights in Poland. Some feminists describe this as a backlash in reaction to the advances in women's rights (as a result of the efforts of the women's movement).

both men and women still have self-censorship mechanisms about their own roles in society

A part of this conundrum is that we are still deeply connected to centuries-old gender stereotypes (that are very hard to change) and both men and women still have self-censorship mechanisms about their own roles in society. As Marion Debruyne (Dean of the Vlerick Business School) argues: "Women embed the expectations on roles. And since there are still few women leaders, there is a lot of room for pigeon-holing. When there will be more women, there will also be more freedom – i.e. there will be many different ways in which a woman can lead. Not just 'like a woman' which falls into stereotypes again..."

To move forward we need to remain focused, developing long-term strategies and resilience to deal with setbacks and work towards changes in mentalities. Women remain today leaders for inclusion and equality.

3. Real Change Towards Equality Requires Courage and Awareness

Contesting gender roles requires awareness, determination, and courage for both women and men. It often requires breaking new ground to create partnerships. And while Brussels might provide a certain space of freedom, as we saw in the stories set out in this book, Brussels is still shaped by the trends and traditional cultural norms of EU member states – not to mention the human preference to avoid risks and to follow familiar patterns instead of embracing change. The three core EU institutions (Commission, European Council and Parliament) are headed by men (Juncker, Tusk, Tajani), as are NATO and most multinational bodies; conferences and summits are dominated by men; unconscious bias and blatantly sexist policies determine hiring processes for senior positions around town; and the tendency to be valued by seniority and professional affiliation, as well as the traditional cultural norms of member states make Brussels a conservative environment. In today's uncertain world, enabling women to more actively pursue professional advancement and reach leadership positions cannot be tackled without reflecting deeply on the implications for men, institutional structures and society at large – and acting consistently and boldly at a systemic level.

So how does one do this in the international Brussels context, a space that brings together the differences of 28 EU member states (as this book goes to press, the UK has only just opened negotiations to leave the EU) as well as all the other countries that gather here? How does an individual speak up and lead in an environment where institutions in the various professional sectors have grown accustomed to operating in certain ways and according to traditional roles and mindsets?

There are no quick fixes in any of the sectors in Brussels and this kind of systemic change cannot be expected overnight. Moreover, explaining Brussels and its multiple "bubbles" and power dynamics in a simple model is impossible. There are too many levels of decision-making, too many actors, multiple power centres and no single-leader identity. Change requires long term commitment, powerful role models, the courage of transformational leadership and vision. We are all actors of change, as individuals and, when possible, as decision-makers in our institutions. We have included, in Part IV, some suggestions to initiate change.

4. Men Remain Untapped Resources in Ending Gender Inequality

Gender parity refers to an equal contribution of women and men to every dimension of life, private or public. However, the topic is mostly discussed from the perspective of women's situations and aspirations in society. Men are "unused capital" in ending gender inequality in the professional context (JUMP Forum, 2015).

Men are "unused capital" in ending gender inequality

Reflection on what "gender diversity" and "gender parity" mean for men, for their careers, professional advancement, and their lives in general is only slowly emerging. In most organisations today, the role of men in diversity and inclusion efforts often remains unexamined, which has consequences that can disrupt or derail the best planned activities aimed at increasing the variety of talents and backgrounds in teams, and getting this mix to work well together (what HR professionals refer to as "Diversity & Inclusion" initiatives). There are rarely occasions to discuss how traditional gender roles also reduce men's freedom to choose a lifestyle that suits them. What are the needs of working fathers in Brussels? Men rarely get asked the question how they manage the work life / family life balance. Figures show they tend not to use their paternity rights and privileges (European Investment Bank, 2016). Yet, reality shows that more men are actually looking for alternatives, especially divorced fathers or men who wish to break from the previous mould of being narrowly defined as the breadwinner.

Anecdotal stories and multiple individual cases make a slow-moving evolution visible to our eyes: the male manager who takes full paternity leave; the working father who rushes to work in the morning after he has dropped off his child at day care; the Member of the European Parliament who declines a prestigious committee position to spend more quality time with his 16-year old son; the father who does the weekly shopping with his kids while his wife speaks at a big event; the EC Head of Unit who is a strong defender of gender diversity even if he has had to compete with women for senior postings and did not advance as quickly as he might once have expected – something that makes many of his peers feel threatened; the supervisor who encourages a woman among his staff to apply for a senior position and backs her with a strong recommendation; the senior staff member in an EU institution who engages in a mentoring programme for women. These are men who do things differently but they do not brag about it and there is no public mentioning of them yet.

5. Men on the Move

There is still great ambivalence among many men (and some women) towards gender equality. And for lasting change to happen, men need to first recognise that inequality exists. As a pioneer in inspiring men to become full diversity partners, Bill Proudman, founding partner and CEO of White Men as Full Diversity Partners, says: "It is ironic that diversity work has focused on the needs of every group while ignoring white men, arguably, the most influential group in affecting transformation in the workplace. The net effect is many white men do not see how diversity and inclusion efforts are about them and their group. This suggests to white men that their efforts are not only, not about them, but that they have everything to lose from the gain of others."

The way towards parity includes having more men realise that they do not automatically lose out when inclusion and diversity become "normal", but that instead this can also be a win-win situation for them. However, this realisation is not yet a reality. Many men actually do feel like they lose out as senior positions and associated status become less available to them. We need to recognise that, while developing new options and choices for men as well.

The new narrative for men gained momentum in the US after Anne-Marie Slaughter's husband wrote his article "Why I Put My Wife's Career First" (The Atlantic, October 2015), sharing his side of the story of when his wife headed Policy Planning at the US Department of State. Andrew Moravcsik, Professor of Politics and director of the European Union Program at Princeton University, spoke in Brussels in 2015 on the topic of being a new type of working father who did the lion's share of caring for the children and took care of domestic affairs as well as worked – something new for this city. We have yet to hear more husbands and partners of professionally successful women share their stories and become alternative role models. For gender roles to evolve and consistently adapt to the new reality of talented professional women wanting to be part of the spheres of power, and men wanting to spend more quality time with their families, there is a need for each of us to re-invent for ourselves what a sustainable and satisfactory life is and what "success" means.

there is a need for each of us to re-invent for ourselves what "success" means

Curious to shed some light on the Brussels "male perspective" on these issues, we surveyed 80 men from the public sector (35), civil society (23, including foundations, media, think tanks, research institutions and advocacy organisations), and the private sector (22). The men surveyed represented most of the EU member states. Some of the questions we asked them were similar to those we asked women interviewees. The survey results revealed awareness about the lack of gender equality, yet also an uncertainty – whether to move towards more parity and/or how this change mattered to men. Men's responses to the question "can men and women have it all?" equally revealed a struggle to adapt their (professional and personal) lives to achieve balance. While there is goodwill and many men say they do their share at home, many confess that their partners still do more. This is supported by recent data from EIGE that shows that women do 22 hours unpaid work per week versus 9 for men. For example, in France men's contribution to unpaid domestic work has increased just 2 minutes per day in the past decade.

Similarly to the women we interviewed, many men were reluctant to say there were gender-specific differences in leadership styles. Most stated that leadership differences were more dependent on individual characteristics than on gender identity. As one respondent said: "Having had both male and female superiors, I can't really say that the gender had much to do with the differences. Character and experience are what set them apart." Yet, some recognise that men and women are judged differently in the way they lead or in the way they are perceived as qualified for a job.

Despite this apparent trend towards openness, most men still struggle with the notion of quotas. In general, they prefer to invest in specific female candidates that show potential rather than support quotas. Having said this, many men defend the creation of working environments that promote balance between professional life and private life for both genders.

Research shows that it is often men in middle management who hinder women's promotion or do not engage in ways to promote female colleagues ("Do Men Want Equality in the Workplace", Jump Forum, 2015). It becomes evident that resistance to change is one of the root causes for setbacks. It requires tremendous effort to go beyond conventional roles, perceptions and responsibilities. Many men are pulled by two opposing forces: on the one hand, they fear losing their traditional role, standing and career privileges; on the other, they intimately feel the heavy burden of commonly having to be the main breadwinner. Yet, what still seems to be absent is sensitivity to how women are held back by deeply ingrained, traditional gender roles that started from an early age and cannot be changed overnight.

6. In Brussels, Influence Happens in Multiple Forms

As a structured first look at the reality of women's leadership in the capital of Europe, in this book we focus on formal leadership. However, we remain convinced of the importance of *informal* leadership, as long as there is a vision, influence, passion and a collective goal. We have come to see this as a type of leadership that is very common among women in Brussels. It is easier to access, less contested, grows organically, but is nevertheless based on knowledge and understanding of the city's dynamics and can have real impact.

we remain convinced of the importance of informal leadership

Leading new initiatives, organising networks, speaking up in debates within a professional sector or across sectors, bringing together different types of stakeholders, or spearheading content-oriented projects to further a cause – all these have enabled women in Brussels to move things forward and gain visibility and influence. While women develop their careers and seek more formal leadership roles, sometimes informal ways, in which they can contribute to the changes they want to see happening, allow them to practise their leadership.

The very concept of leadership should be seen as less rigid than having a formal senior role in a hierarchy: "Leadership is a process of social influence, which maximises the efforts of others, towards the achievement of a goal." (Forbes, 2013). Therefore, while you go through the different stages of your career, there are multiple opportunities to get engaged in initiatives beyond the confinements of a paid job – to contribute towards change and exert an influence that is consistent with your vision and values. A city like Brussels is full of these opportunities but they are still disproportionately used by men, because of systemic barriers and uneven burden of unpaid family care. So influence and leadership start at home!

7. The Vibrant World of Brussels' Women's Networks and Support Initiatives

As one respondent to our men's survey said: "As well as a strong set of skills in Brussels, it takes a great ability to cultivate and maintain interpersonal relationships and great emotional intelligence." In Brussels, a rich "contacts list" is one of the keys for success. Networks, alliances and specialised support services and organisations are crucial to effectively operate and thrive in the complex mesh of power dynamics, both for men and women professionals. Networking is part of today's professional reality for most people. Men have always used business trips, conferences, after-work drinks, sports getaways to build professional capital strategically. Women, on the other hand, are generally considered not to spend enough time on professional networking – partly because many still perceive it as difficult, not useful and as time not spent efficiently, as well as a barrier to spending time with their families or friends. Consequently, they spend more time "doing" and less time "networking." As Carol Bartz, former CEO of Yahoo, says: "Women's lack of access to informal networks is a structural obstacle to their career advancement, comparable in impact to lacking a mentor, or appropriate coaching and training." (Fortune, 2014).

> *Men have always used business trips, conferences, after-work drinks, sports getaways to build professional capital strategically*

Brussels accommodates a variety of associations, networks, events, programmes, coaches, mentors and initiatives that might be of use to you, and new initiatives continue to emerge as we write. We have carried out a first mapping of them, the results of which can be found in Part IV. The sheer variety of initiatives and organisations shows the vibrancy and engagement of women of all ages who are behind these initiatives – as well as the demand.

There are a wide range of initiatives and networks aligned around sectors (e.g. entrepreneurship, public policy, political participation, media, etc.), around national identities and specific institutions (such as the European Commission and NATO), and around professional interests and specific objectives – be it trade, security, competition or professional development. All of them play an important role in helping women achieve their professional goals – e.g. managing current job responsibilities, accessing information, boosting professional development, or providing the space for strategic collaboration focused on new directions and contact with other stakeholders. While the large number of networks, institutions, associations, and formal and informal groups of women might be seen as creating too much competition with each other, perceived competitors can also become allies, when they share a common agenda and they manage to find synergies around common values and goals. The challenge is to know who is "out there" and what they do and seek synergies and collaboration, such as helping each other to amplify one's voice for a particular cause or objective.

Making Gender Equality the New Normal …

Women in Brussels are slowly continuing their journey to access all professional sectors and levels. Progress is being made in spite of the pervasive resistance of those privileged by the status quo, widespread (conscious and unconscious) bias, and women's own occasional hesitation to embrace opportunities. We can observe emerging "communities" of excellent, self-confident women role models, bold women who lead in different ways, change organisational systems and are dynamic actors of social, political and economic change. These are women who are transforming the system!

We can observe emerging "communities" of excellent, self-confident women role models

Despite this, gender equality is far from the rule. It is evident that the next steps towards genuine diversity at the top are tough and challenging. Sustainable systemic change requires determination, creativity, vision, courage and lots of networking. It also involves careful strategies, long term engagement, and systematic monitoring. Significantly, it requires compilation of and access to more reliable and comparable data – for example, during our research we realised there was a data gap in some specific Brussels-based sectors (e.g. NGOs, foundations, think tanks, etc.). It is evident that better and more comprehensive data would help to challenge traditional mindsets, and assist decision-makers to gain a real understanding of their own services and organisations. And when data exists, it is important to make it visible and influence those taking decisions.

… In Brussels, in Europe and Elsewhere

We believe diversity of voices, styles and views is particularly critical in the historical moment we are living – where Europe and its existence as a project for collaboration is under stress, calling for renewal and modernisation. Diversity must be at its core during this modernisation process.

We also believe that the EU project makes more sense today than ever. The geopolitical context is one of widespread instability and unpredictability, climate change and increasing lack of resources in an over-populated planet; there is the forthcoming impact of artificial intelligence on labour and societies; and there are the threats from the rise of extremists and populists, poverty, and regional conflicts, among many others. These big challenges require a complex and collaborative approach to leadership in the coming years. This world of today requires the courageous leadership of a functioning EU; of an EU that can galvanise citizens and member states again with a powerful vision to guide the upcoming decades.

The EU we need today is (still) a project where human rights and equality are not just nice concepts, but a lived reality – where diversity is not perceived as charity nor as a secondary agenda and where actions replace words. A Europe that understands fully that no country or region can truly progress if it suppresses the potential of its citizens and deprives itself of the talent and contributions of half of its population.

The EU we want must reflect the complexity and variety of its citizens. In an age of inter-dependence, this regional reform needs to be inclusive, comprehensive and to acknowledge that today's problems require collaboration – among different sectors (private and public, political and policy, civil society and media), different countries, different communities, different people from diverse backgrounds. We believe that this complex multi-layer collaboration is key to finding innovative policies and modern solutions to the problems we face today and tomorrow; to enable a sustainable and agile work force to contribute to the comfort and security of our societies; and to the collective sense of stability and hope we need to inculcate in Europe's citizens.

In the Europe we want, women will lead from the front

In the Europe we want, women will lead from the front and not from behind. This Europe will promote a leadership culture which pushes forward talent, and challenges privilege based on gender, age and race. It will be a Europe that makes a sustainable future and diversity a major strategic objective, truly integrated into institutional strategies and daily life, in schools and in all sectors of our society – so that one day, diversity becomes the new standard.

PART IV

RESOURCES
FOR CHANGE-MAKERS

In Part IV we provide some ideas and information that can help you develop yourself and your organisation, get connected and feel supported.

The first chapter has our recommendations of ideas to drive change towards more gender-diverse cultures.

The second is an inventory of organisations, networks and initiatives that support women's professional empowerment in Brussels.

Following Part IV, Annex I gives our suggestions for further reading if you wish to explore any of the topics in the book. Annex II provides a short glossary of some of the more important terms on gender and leadership issues that you are likely to encounter.

Recommendations to Increase Gender Diversity

Start with Awareness

Awareness is frequently triggered by personal experiences. For example, an "incident" can bring an individual to question the traditional gender status quo – discovering that a male peer receives a bigger salary for the same job; realising that there are systematically more men speaking at conferences and white men dominating executive levels at work; getting pregnant and being fired; a woman being considered too fragile to go on a mission to an insecure country; being more harshly criticised than male peers for the same decision, and so on. As Iris Bohnet notes in her widely acclaimed book "What Works", striving for equality between men and women starts with awareness that "our minds are stubborn beasts".

we all see "reality" based on our personal beliefs, conventions and expectations

Here then are some concrete tips on how to increase (individual and organisational) awareness in a more purposeful manner:

1. Realise that we are all biased and that is simply the way our brain works: we all see "reality" based on our personal beliefs, conventions and expectations. Find out your "blind spots" and test yourself for unconscious bias (e.g. with the free online test developed by Harvard's Project Implicit). Seek opportunities to speak and work with people who are different/think differently to you – exchange with and learn from them. When you think you no longer fall into stereotyping, be aware that this is itself a blind spot. Regularly question your assumptions and judgements.
2. Have discussions at work about gender rather than women/women's issues. Discuss roles and relationship between men and women, e.g. working parents, pay gaps, unconscious bias; acknowledge and appreciate differences. Signal to men that their perspectives on gender issues are valued.
3. Ask your executive or management team to include gender awareness programmes and to use these as a part of the performance review process

of your employer. If you are in a sector where performance review is not common practice, ask for it.

4. Be attentive and raise other people's awareness of the subtle ways in which some people unconsciously cause women colleagues to feel diminished (e.g. interrupting them, reading messages or papers when women speak, leaving the room, appropriating their suggestions and ideas as if they were theirs, etc.).

Cultivate Systemic Change

Awareness is fundamental, but it is not enough to change structures and systems. For performance to match good intentions, more needs to be done, as we have discussed in multiple sections of this book. Many sources agree that one key objective must be to build a critical mass of at least 30% of women at all levels of the organisation (board, executive level, advisory committees) to ensure that diverse views are given a voice.

Awareness is fundamental, but it is not enough to change structures

So far, programmes adopted by organisations to advance women have included mentoring, networking, coaching, maternity leave, child care benefits, and flexible work options. But these efforts are treating symptoms. "Real diversity efforts require organizations to address the cultural and social patterns that suppress women's careers, not just the symptoms that result from them. Diversity and inclusion efforts need to attack the inherent systemic biases and assumptions that come into play millions of times a day, in localised ways, and that are inadvertently supported by legacy policies and procedures. (…) Organizations need to enable very different types of dialogue so that local teams can change themselves and reshape how policies affect their members." (Harvard Business Review, February 2017).

Here are some specific tips for advancing organisational change and going beyond just "checking the boxes".

1. While sometimes the change impetus starts at mid-management level and/or with engaged human resources actors, it is important to engage the top executive level, as soon as possible, and make decision-makers accountable for developing and promoting this transformational process.

2. Important steps in your plan:
    -   Collect hard data. Audit your organisation's gendered reality and build a diversity plan tailored to its needs and specific goals. Be clear about what you want to change.
    -   Identify and (re)design your organisation's processes to reduce and prevent biased choices.
    -   Define gender targets, policies and programmes (hiring, promotion, compensation policies, training, mentoring, coaching, performance review benchmarks, work-life flexibility opportunities, etc.) that are consistent with previous steps and with the uniqueness of your organisation. Measure and document the impact over time.
    -   Reform recruitment and talent management, where biases are widespread. Whenever possible, use hard data instead of intuitive processes, and use software that allow employers to blind themselves to applicants' demographic characteristics so you can concentrate on talent only.
    -   Implement a culture of zero tolerance on sexual harassment, gender discrimination and sexism, based on clear rules, transparent processes and accountability.
    -   Track the progress of women at all levels in your organisation over time, and monitor development. Re-adapt programmes, whenever this is needed.
    -   Communicate expectations, targets, day-to-day evidence and achievements. Publicly reward managers for making progress on inclusion and diversity goals.

Here are a few easy-to-implement habits to engrain in your daily working life which can have a huge impact.

1. Hold meetings and conference calls only during office hours.
2. Check if you have gender diverse teams, meetings, events, panels, grantees, partners and stakeholders. Ensure diversity in the images and language you use in your communications.
3. In job interviews and evaluations, be alert to potentially biased language.
4. Put pictures of women role models in the office – the closer these models are to your organisational values and culture, the more effective an impact this initiative will have.

All the recommendations above can be used in and adapted to organisations in the different sectors discussed in this book. In events and discussions in Brussels, the private sector is already regularly sharing lessons learnt, difficulties and setbacks, as well as good practices – but more sharing across sectors could be done.

Contributing to Systemic Change as Individuals

As individuals, we are also part of change processes. Here are a few tips that both men and women can make use of as individuals, depending on their roles, specific goals and opportunities. This set of suggestions will be particularly effective when used by those with decision-making authority.

1. Encourage in-house discussion about the benefits of gender equality and of work-life balance for both men and women. Encourage your organisation to include a gender perspective in all its initiatives. Use the suggestions above to prepare better for this.
2. Include women colleagues if you notice them being excluded from conversations/decision-making processes. Make them visible in meetings and other events.
3. Take advantage of work-life flexibility benefits yourself (paternity leave, family leave, tele-commuting, flexitime), but remain visible at important moments at work. If your organisation does not offer these benefits, ask for them for women and men. Communicate your support to male colleagues who use the benefits.
4. Engage in gender reverse mentoring: male supervisors are paired up with and mentored by female colleagues with an eye to spotting gender issues.
5. Mentor/sponsor a woman. Encourage and support a woman in her professional development. But also sponsor her, i.e. advocate for her when she is pursuing new opportunities. Sponsors go beyond the traditional social, emotional, and personal growth development provided by many mentors. Sponsorship is the active support by someone appropriately placed in the system who has significant influence on decision-making processes or structures and who is advocating for, protecting, and fighting for the career advancement of an individual (Ibarra et al., Harvard Business Review, September 2010).
6. Challenge gender-biased language or behaviour.
7. Show zero tolerance to sexual harassment and sexism: ask for transparent policies and implementation mechanisms. Denounce breaches of this rule. Do not engage in sexist jokes, even if they sound "normal" in certain cultures.

8. Promote and praise (gender) diverse teams, panels, meetings, etc. When appropriate, consider refusing to be part of unbalanced initiatives.
9. Ask for transparency on salaries and gender balance in hiring and promotions.
10. Ensure that administrative and logistic tasks are not consistently delegated to or assumed by women team members/colleagues.
11. Educate your children about equality and the benefits of (gender) diversity.

The Vibrant World of Brussels Women's Networks and Support Initiatives

In this section, we provide a first inventory of the organisations, networks and initiatives operating in Brussels which support women's professional development in various ways (e.g. organising events, surveys, networking and mentoring opportunities, etc.). The list below is necessarily incomplete as new initiatives and projects are regularly emerging in this exciting city.

A

African Caribbean Pacific Young Professionals Network (ACP YPN)	ACP YPN brings together young professionals and diaspora from Africa, the Caribbean and Pacific, fostering dialogue. While being open to men and women, its leadership and membership is predominantly female.
Amazone Belgium – Crossroads for Women's Organizations, Gender Equality	Amazone aims to create synergies and join the forces of the women's movement. It hosts the offices of nearly twenty women's organizations and has a Documentation Centre on Gender Policy.
AmCham EU "Gender Initiatives Task Force"	The Task Force provides a discussion and networking platform for members of AmCham EU on topics related to gender and diversity.

B

Belgian Women in Science (BeWiSe)	BeWiSe supports the position of women in science, in both the public and private sectors. Their reach goes beyond Belgium and their programme includes events and mentoring for women in science.

Brussels Countess Markievicz Circle	The Countess Markievicz Circle's original mission was to support "Women for Election" in Ireland. They are currently exploring ways to becoming a "European Women for Elections" endeavour.
Brussels Pioneers	Brussels Pioneers provides technical support and guidance to women with a business project in Brussels.
BrusselsNV – Network of Dutch Women in Brussels	BrusselsNV is a network of Dutch women in or around the European Institutions. By connecting, training and empowering women, BrusselsNV assists women in their career advancement.
Brux-Elles	Brux-Elles is an informal network of female journalists from different countries. They regularly organise background briefings with EU actors.

C

Cercle Olympe Brussels	Cercle Olympe is a network of women and a platform for exchanges on societal topics, bringing together both Belgian professional women and women working in "international Brussels".
Club L Benelux	Club L Benelux is a socially prestigious club for women from the Belgian establishment. Some of them hold senior roles in various fields of Belgian society.
College of Europe Alumni Women's Group	CoE Alumni Women is a network of young professionals who are keen on advancing gender equality in the workplace.

D

Digital African Woman (DAW) – Brussels branch	DAW encourages young girls to explore careers in tech industries and supports female-led start-ups from the African diaspora and the African continent.

Digital Leadership Institute (DLI)	DLI promotes greater participation of girls and women in strategic, innovative ESTEAM sectors.

E

Equinet – European Network of Equality Bodies	Equinet brings together 46 equality bodies (independent organisations established on the basis of EU equal treatment directives) from 34 European countries.
EU Panel Watch	EU Panel Watch is a campaign to promote more diversity in panels and debates.
European Forum of Muslim Women (EFOMW)	EFOMW supports Muslim women within society and defends their rights and opportunities at the European and International level.
European Institute for Gender Equality (EIGE)	EIGE is an autonomous institution of the EU, based in Vilnius. It is a knowledge centre on gender equality issues. Among other things, it provides: (i) an annual gender equality index assessing the impact of gender equality policies in the EU and its member states; and (ii) a Euro Gender network, an online cooperation and consultation hub that allows all its members to share knowledge and contribute to advancing gender equality in Europe and beyond.
European Network of Female Policy Experts / The Brussels Binder	This is an informal network promoting the role of women in think tanks and policy debate. The Brussels Binder was established as a crowdfunding initiative to build an online database of female policy experts in Brussels.
European Network of Migrant Women (ENOMW)	ENOMW represents the views of migrants, refugee women and girls at the European and international level.
European Women Alliance (EWA)	EWA is an incipient initiative aiming to contribute to increasing women's voices in policy debates related to the the European project. Members are mostly from the European Parliament.

European Women Alliance (EWA)	EWA is an incipient initiative aiming to contribute to increasing women's voices in policy debates related to the the European project. Members are mostly from the European Parliament.
European Women Lawyers Association (EWLA)	EWLA is a federation of national women lawyers' associations from EU countries and the European Free Trade Association (EFTA) countries.
European Women on Boards – EWoB	A partially EU funded project aimed at bringing together various national/EU member state initiatives to increase the number of women on boards. They have produced a first online pool of selected women ready for boards.
European Women's Lobby (EWL)	EWL is the largest European umbrella network of women's associations, representing more than 2,000 organisations in all EU member states and candidate countries, as well as 19 European-wide organisations representing the diversity of women and girls in Europe. Through events, mentoring programmes, research/surveys and other initiatives, they bring together the women's movements in Europe to influence the public and European Institutions in support of women's human rights and equality between women and men.
European Women's Management Development International Network (EWMD)	EWMD is an international network for women and men in management which links professionals from different fields.
Expertalia	Expertalia.be is a Belgian initiative aiming at making women more visible in the media and supporting more inclusive reporting.

F

French women in the European Commission	An informal network among French women in the European Commission aiming to provide support and exchange.

G

Gender 5+	The first independent European Feminist Think Tank. Affiliates participate in research, public debates and consultations.
Gentlewomen's Club	The Gentlewomen's Club is a young women's initiative focusing on professional support through networking. It encourages non-stereotypical behaviour.
German women in management positions in the European Commission	This group forms an informal network in the European Commission promoting mutual support and exchange among women.
Greenlight for Girls	Greenlight for Girls is an international organisation which encourages girls to pursue STEM subjects.

I

INSEAD Women in Business	INSEAD aims to accelerate gender balance towards a more inclusive, innovative leadership and culture in organisations worldwide.
Interface3	Interface3, a Belgian initiative, works to support women in administration and IT careers.

J

JUMP	JUMP aims to close the gap between women and men at work, achieve sustainable corporate performance and create a more equal society. They organise an annual JUMP Forum in Brussels, as well as other events, trainings and surveys on the topics of gender diversity and inclusion in Europe.

L

LEAD@COMM	A network for women 'Administrators' (ADs) in the European Commission, assisting talented women in their professional development and career progression.
Leadarise, Brussels chapter	Leadarise is an international network inspiring young women professionals and entrepreneurs to maximise their leadership impact.
League of Badass Women (LOBAW), Brussels chapter	LOBAW is an informal women's gathering involving women from diverse sectors exploring and nurturing more feminist activism amongst them.

M

Millennia2015 Women and Innovation Foundation	Millennia2015, now also known as Millennia2025, focuses on using foresight research and information technology to empower more women over the next decade.
Mizbiz	Mizbiz is a network for female professionals from various industries and is built around three core values: connect, inspire & empower women.

N

NATO Women's Professional Network (NWPN)	The NATO Women's Professional Network is part of the NATO Mentoring Programme. It serves as a digital platform for women who have gone through the mentoring programmes, and other women at NATO, to exchange information and ideas on women & gender-relevant topics.

P

Professional Women International Brussels (PWI)	PWI is a Brussels-based multinational networking forum for women in all professional sectors providing a forum for interaction. They organise regular networking events and debates, and organise one of the first mentoring programmes in town.

S

Soroptimist International (SI), Brussels chapters	SI is a network based on philanthropic principles, geared to support and to empower women and girls world wide.
SWAN, a pillar of the SAIS Women Lead (SWL) Initiative	SWAN aims to position SAIS alumnae as leaders in international relations and related fields by hosting a diverse line-up of activities.

T

The Sofia Foundation	The Sofia Foundation support initiatives that accelerate women's participation in economic, political and social governance across Europe.

U

UN Women, Brussels office	UN Women is the UN organisation dedicated to gender equality and the empowerment of women.

W

Women@	Women@ is a platform which aims to help women professionals' presence in public space.
Women Business Angels	Women Business Angels for Europe's Entrepreneurs (WA4E), an EU-funded project, promotes and professionalises female investment in 6 countries: Belgium, France, Italy, Portugal, Spain and the UK. This initiative is part of the European Confederation of Angel Investing.

Women Entrepreneurship Platform (WEP)	The WEP in Brussels brings together like-minded organisations of women entrepreneurs or women in business, keeping both national and European associations of women entrepreneurs abreast of happenings at EU level.
Women in Business	Women in Business strives to create a better understanding of female entrepreneurial dynamics in Brussels and to shed light on existing initiatives.
Women in Civil Society	Affiliated with the European Women's Lobby (EWL), this informal group includes women leaders from different NGOs in Brussels.
Women in Development Europe (WIDE+)	Wide+ is a space to network and multiply the impact of feminist activism in the Development Cooperation sector.
Women in International Security (WIIS), Brussels chapter	WIIS Brussels promotes women in the international relations, security and defence fields. WIIS offers professional development, networking and policy discussion opportunities.
Women in Leadership (WIL), Brussels chapter	WIL's purpose is to offer European senior professional women an intimate platform to discuss, exchange, and network to develop their full leadership potential.
Women In Trade Network (WTN), Brussels	A network of women from different sectors working on international trade. Their meetings promote proactive engagement of women in topics related to global trade.
Women Political Leaders Global Forum (WPL)	The Women Political Leaders Global Forum (WPL) is a global network of female politicians. WPL's mission is to increase the number and influence of women in political leadership positions. Their Women European Leaders (WEL) community in Brussels serves as an inter-institutional platform for women leaders in the European Institutions to discuss issues that are high on the international agenda, as well as their personal leadership journeys.

Women's Competition Network (WCN)	WCN is the international women's network for senior competition law and policy professionals to promote the advancement of women in the field.

Y

Young Feminist Europe	Young Feminist Europe is a network of feminist people in Europe, based in Brussels. It aims to meet the political and social/recreational needs of the wider community of diverse young feminists in Europe.

Annex I

Our Personal Suggestions for Learning More

Leadership and Women in Leadership

ADICHIE, Chimamanda Ngozi, *We Should All Be Feminists*, New York: Anchor Books, 2014

AUSTIN, Linda Gong, *What's Holding You Back? Eight Critical Choices for Women's Success*, New York: Basic Books, 2000

BABCOCK, Linda and LASCHEVER, Sarah, *Women Don't Ask: Negotiation and the Gender Divide*, Princeton: Princeton University Press, 2003

BARSH, Joanna, CRANSTON, Susie and LEWIS, Geoffrey, *How Remarkable Women Lead: The Breakthrough Model for Work and Life*, New York: Crown Business, 2011

BEARD, Alison, "Mary Robinson on Influence Without Authority," *Harvard Business Review*, Feb. 21, 2013

BEAUVOIR, Simone de, *The Second Sex*, New York: Vintage Publishing, 2010

BOHNET, Iris, *What Works: Gender Equality by Design*, Harvard University Press, 2016

BRADBERRY, Travis and GREAVES, Jean, *Emotional Intelligence 2.0.*, San Diego: Talentsmart, 2009

BRANSON, Douglas, *No Seat at the Table: How Corporate Governance and Law Keep Women Out of the Boardroom*, New York: New York University Press, 2007

BUFLENS, Marc and DE STOBBELEIR, Katleen, *Grandmaster in Leadership*, Ghent: Vlerick Leuven Gent Management School, 2009

BURNS, James MacGregor, *Transforming Leadership*, New York: Grove Press, 2003

CHALEFF, Ira, *Intelligent Disobedience: Doing Right When You're Told to Do Wrong*, Oakland: Berrett-Koehler, 2015

CHALEFF, Ira, *The Courageous Follower: Standing Up to and for Our Leader*s, Oakland: Berrett-Koehler, 2009

DREHER, Diane, *The Tao of Womanhood: Ten Lessons for Power and Peace*, New York: HarperCollins Publishers, 1999

EAGLY, Alice H. and CARLI, Linda L., *Through the Labyrinth: The Truth About How Women Become Leaders*, Harvard: Harvard Business School Press, 2007

FRIEDAN, Betty, *The Feminine Mystique*, London: Penguin Books Ltd, 2010

GATTI, Emanuele, "Defining the Expat: The Case of High-Skilled Migrants in Brussels," *Brussels Studies*, 2009

GOLEMAN, Daniel, *Emotional Intelligence: Why It Can Matter More Than IQ*, New York: Bantam, 1995

GOLEMAN, Daniel, *Focus: The Hidden Driver of Excellence*, New York: HarperCollins Publishers, 2013

HARRIS, Lynn, *Unwritten Rules: What Women Need to Know About Leading in Today's Organizations*, n.p.: Lyn Harris, 2009

IBARRA, Herminia, *Act Like a Leader, Think Like a Leader*, Harvard: Harvard Business School Publishing, 2015

IBARRA, Herminia and CARTER Nancy M. and SILVA Christine, "Why Men Still Get More Promotions Than Women," *Harvard Business Review*, 2010, pp. 80-85

JOHNSON, Tory and SPIZMAN, Robyn Freedman, *Women for Hire's Get-Ahead Guide to Career Success*, New York: The Berkley Publishing Group, 2004

KOLB, Deborah M., WILLIAMS, Judith and FROHLINGER, Carol, *Her Place at the Table: A Woman's Guide to Negotiating Five Key Challenges to Leadership Success*, San Francisco: John Wiley & Sons, 2010

MAXWELL, John C., *5 Levels of Leadership, The Proven Steps to Maximize Your Potential*, New York: Center Street, 2011

MELINA, Lois Ruskai, BURGESS, Gloria J., LID-FALKMAN, Lena and MARTURANO, Antonio, editors, *The Embodiment of Leadership: A Volume in the International Leadership Series*, Hoboken: Jossey-Bass, 2013

MILLER, Lee E. and MILLER, Jessica, *A Woman's Guide to Successful Negotiating: How to Convince, Collaborate and Create Your Way to Agreement*, New York: McGraw Hill, 2010

MORAVSCIK, Andrew, "Why I Put My Wife's Career First", *The Atlantic*, Oct. 2015

O'REILLY, Nancy D., *Leading Women: 20 Influential Women Share Their Secrets to Leadership, Business, and Life*, Avon: Adams Media, 2014

RUDERMAN, Marian N. and OHLOTT, Patricia J., *Standing at the Crossroads: Next Steps for High-Achieving Women*, San Francisco: John Wiley & Sons, 2002

SANDBERG, Sheryl, *Lean In: Women, Work, and the Will to Lead*, New York: Alfred A. Knopf, 2013

SCHUYLER, Kathryn Goldman, BAUGHER John Eric and JIRONET, Karin, editors, *Creative Social Change: Leadership for a Healthy World*, Bradford: Emerald Publishing, 2016

SCUMACI, Dondi, *Designed For Success: The 10 Commandments for Women in the Workplace*, Lake Mary: Excel Books, 2007

SLAUGHTER, Anne-Marie, "Why Women Still Can't Have it All", *The Atlantic*, Jul./Aug. 2012

SLAUGHTER, Anne-Marie, *Unfinished Business: Women, Men, Work, Family*, New York: Random House, 2015

SOFER, Catherine, "Inégalités de genre. Hommes et femmes au travail et dans la famille. Lire l'interview", *SorbonnEco*, 15 Apr. 2014

SHEPARD, Molly D, STIMMLER, Jane K. and DEAN, Peter, *Breaking into the Boy's Club: 8 Ways for Women to Move Ahead in Business*, Plymouth: Rowman & Littlefield, 2014

VALENTI, Jessica, *Full Frontal Feminism: A Young Woman's Guide to Why Feminism Matters*, Emeryville: Seal Press, 2014

Brussels and Europe

BAETEN, Guy, "The Europeanization of Brussels and the Urbanization of 'Europe'", *European Urban and Regional Studies*, vol. 8, no. 2, pp. 117-130

BECKER, Markus and MULLER, Peter, "Why Belgium Keeps Popping Up in Terror Attacks", *Spiegel Online*, 16 Nov. 2015

Brussels Studies, https://brussels.revues.org/245

CORIJN, Eric, and VANDERMOTTEN, Christian, DECROLY, Michel and SWYNGEDOUW, Erik, "Brussels as an International City", *Brussels Studies*, no. 13, 2009

DEBOOSERE, Patrick and EGGERICKX, Thierry, VAN HECKE, Etienne and WAYENS, Benjamin, "The Population of Brussels: a Demographic Overview", *Brussels Studies*, no. 3, 2009

ERIKSSON, Alexandra, and TKATCH, Daniel, "Integrating Europeans into Multi-Cultural Brussels", *EUObserver*, 14 Apr. 2015

HARDING, Gareth, "The Golden Cage of Brussels", *garethharding*, n.d., http://garethharding.com/ the-golden-cage-of-brussels

NIELSEN, Nikolaj, "Molenbeek Locals Counter 'Terrorist Image' with Vigil", *EUObserver*, 18 Nov. 2015

TUAL, Morgane, "Vu de Bruxelles : « Tout le monde était un peu parano, mais là ça va mieux »", *Le Monde*, 25 Nov. 2015

WISE, Michael Z., "Think Tank; A Capital of Europe? Brussels Is Primping", *The New York Times*, 2 Mar. 2002

Gender and Feminism

Feminist Studies, University of Maryland, http://wmst.umd.edu

Gender in Management: An International Journal, Emerald Insight, 2017,
http://www.emeraldinsight.com/journal/gm

Gender & Society (Official journal of Sociologists for Women in Society),
Sage Journal, 2017, http://journals.sagepub.com/home/gas

Gender, Work and Organization, Keele University,
https://www.keele.ac.uk/humssr/journals/gwo

Journal of Women, Politics & Policy, Taylor & Francis Online (Routledge), 2017,
http://www.tandfonline.com/loi/wwap20

International Journal of Gender and Entrepreneurship, Emerald Insight, 2017,
http://www.emeraldinsight.com/journal/ijge

The Leadership Quarterly, Elsevier, 2017,
https://www.journals.elsevier.com/the-leadership-quarterly

Women in Management Review, Emerald Insight, 2017,
http://www.emeraldinsight.com/loi/wimr

Women & Leadership: Research, Theory, and Practice Book Series,
International Leadership Association (ILA).
http://www.ila-net.org/Publications/WL/index.htm

The Work of the European Institutions in Relevant Areas

EIGE, *Economic Benefits of Gender Equality in the European Union*,
http://eige.europa.eu/gender-mainstreaming/policy-areas/economic-and-
financial-affairs/economic-benefits-gender-equality

EIGE, EIGE's Publications,
http://eige.europa.eu/rdc/eige-publications?a[]=616

EIGE, Toolkits, http://eige.europa.eu/gender-mainstreaming/toolkits

EUROPEAN COMMISSION, DG Justice and Consumers.
http://ec.europa.eu/justice/gender-equality

EUROPEAN COMMISSION, *2017 Report on Equality Between Women and Men in the EU*. European Union, 2017

EUROPEAN PARLIAMENT, Women's Rights and Gender Equality Committee.
http://www.europarl.europa.eu/committees/en/femm/home.html

EUROPEAN PARLIAMENT, *Empowering women in the EU and beyond: Leadership and Conflict Resolution*, EPRS & EUI.
http://www.europarl.europa.eu/RegData/etudes/BRIE/2017/ 599302/EPRS_ BRI(2017)599302_EN.pdf, March 2017

Annex II

Acronyms, Concepts and Jargon

Following is a glossary of acronyms, concepts and jargon. It is divided into two parts. The first is of terms related to gender, the second to leadership.

Gender-related Acronyms, Concepts and Jargon

CEDAW
Convention on the Elimination of All Forms of Discrimination against Women. Also known as the international bill of rights for women. Adopted by the UN General Assembly in 1979 and in force from 1981.

Discrimination against women
Distinction, exclusion or restriction made on the basis of sex and gender that has the effect or purpose of impairing or nullifying the recognition, enjoyment or exercise by women of human rights and fundamental freedoms in the political, economic, social, cultural, civil or any other field.

Equal opportunities
The absence of barriers to economic, political and social participation on grounds of gender. Such barriers are often indirect, difficult to discern and caused and perpetuated by social and economic structures and societal conventions that are resistant to change. Equal opportunities as one of a set of gender equality objectives is founded on the rationale that a whole range of strategies, actions and measures are necessary to redress deep-rooted and persistent inequalities.

Femininity
Social meaning of womanliness, which is constructed and defined socially, historically and politically, rather than being biologically driven. The term relates to perceived notions and ideals about how women should or are expected to behave in a given setting. Femininity is not just about women; men also define its meaning.

Feminism
Belief that men and women should have equal rights and opportunities. It is the theory of the political, economic and social equality of the sexes.

FEMM
Women's Rights and Gender Equality Committee of the European Parliament.

Gender audit
A tool and a process based on a participatory methodology to promote learning at the individual, work unit and organisational levels on how to practically and effectively mainstream gender.

Gender awareness
The ability to view society from the perspective of gender roles and understand how this has affected women's needs in comparison to the needs of men.

Gender "best practices"
Accumulation and application of knowledge about what works and what does not work in terms of promoting gender equality and non-discrimination against women in different contexts. It is about both the lessons learned and the continuing process of learning, feedback, reflection and analysis.

Gender bias
Inclination towards or prejudice against one gender. Bias can be both conscious and unconscious.

Gender blindness
Refers to the failure to recognise that the roles and responsibilities of men/boys and women/girls are assigned to them in specific social, cultural, economic, and political contexts and backgrounds.

Gender diversity
Equitable or fair representation between genders. Gender diversity most commonly refers to an equitable ratio of men and women, but may also include non-binary gender categories.

Gender diversity and inclusion
Diversity is about counting the numbers of men and women at the different levels of organisations. Inclusiveness is about making the numbers count.

Gender equality

Equal rights, responsibilities and opportunities of women and men and girls and boys. Equality does not mean that women and men will become the same but that women's and men's rights, responsibilities and opportunities will not depend on whether they are born male or female.

Gender gap

Any disparity between women's and men's condition or position in society.

Gender identity

Unlike biological sex (assigned at birth and based on physical characteristics) gender identity refers to a person's innate, deeply felt sense of being male or female (sometimes even both or neither).

Gender inequality index (GII)

The index used by the United Nations Development Programme (UNDP) for measuring gender disparity. It measures the loss in human development due to inequality between female and male achievements in three dimensions: (1) reproductive health, (2) empowerment, and (3) the labour market.

Gender mainstreaming

A strategy for implementing greater gender equality in all dimensions and sectors. It is not a goal or objective on its own.

Gender parity

Numerical concept related to gender equality. Working towards gender parity (equal representation of men and women) is a key part of achieving gender equality, and one of the twin strategies, alongside gender mainstreaming.

Gender responsive budgeting (GRB)

An internationally recognised tool that ensures the achievement of de facto gender equality and contributes to the effectiveness of allocation of public funds. GRB brings together two practices that are not commonly associated with one another: gender equality efforts and public finance management.

Gender stereotypes

Simplistic generalisations about the gender attributes, differences and roles of women and men. Stereotypes are both descriptive and prescriptive.

"Glass ceiling"
Metaphor traditionally used to describe a discriminatory barrier which blocks the professional advancement of women (or other groups).

"Glass escalator"
Metaphor used to describe the phenomenon of women trying to climb the ladder, while their male peers glide past them on an invisible escalator, shooting straight to the top.

HeForShe campaign
Solidarity campaign for the advancement of women initiated by UN Women. Its goal is to engage men and boys as agents of change by encouraging them to take action against negative inequalities faced by women and girls.

Masculinity
Social meaning of manhood, which is constructed and defined socially, historically and politically, rather than being biologically driven. The term relates to perceived notions and ideals about how men should or are expected to behave in a given setting. Masculinity is not just about how men perceive themselves; women also define its meaning.

"Manels"
Men-only panels. Also: A male panel of advisors. Primarily used to offer relationship advice to women about men (urban language).

"Mensplaining"
Men explaining (something) to someone, typically a woman, in a manner regarded as condescending or patronising (urban language).

Patriarchy
Traditional form of organising society which often lies at the root of gender inequality.

Quotas
One of the most effective special measures or affirmative actions for increasing women's political participation.

Sexism
Prejudice, stereotyping or discrimination, typically against women, on the basis of sex.

"Sticky floor"
Discriminatory employment patterns that keep a certain group of people at the bottom of the job scale.

UN Women
The "United Nations Entity for Gender Equality and the Empowerment of Women", created in 2010.

Unpaid care work
Encompasses all the daily activities that sustain our lives and health, such as house work and personal care (especially of children, the elderly, people who are sick or have a disability). These activities are most commonly performed by women, for free.

Leadership-related Acronyms, Concepts and Jargon

Authoritarian leadership
A style of leadership in which the leader tells subordinates what needs to be done and how to do it without getting their advice or ideas.

Coaching
Coaching is a process of partnering with clients to maximise their personal and professional potential. It is seen as helping people to learn and develop rather than teaching them.

Decision-making
The process of reaching logical conclusions, solving problems, analysing factual information, and taking appropriate actions based on the conclusions.

Difference between leadership and management
The main difference between leaders and managers is that leaders have people follow them while managers have people who work for them. See "Leadership" and "Management" below.

Diversity and inclusion
Commitment to establishing an environment where the full potential of all employees can be tapped by paying attention to and taking into account their differences in work background, experience, age, gender, race, ethnic origin, physical abilities, religious belief, sexual orientation, and other perceived

differences. Diversity differs from affirmative action, which is more about following laws. Diversity is a range of different people, while inclusion is making them feel welcome and part of the group.

Emotional intelligence (EI)

The capability of individuals to recognise their own and other people's emotions, distinguish between different feelings and label them appropriately, use emotional information to guide thinking and behaviour, and manage and/or adjust emotions to adapt to environments or achieve their goal(s).

Flexitime

Arrangement in which employees are allowed to choose work hours as long as the standard number of work hours and the required results are met.

Inclusive leadership

The practice of leadership that carefully includes the contributions of all stakeholders in the community or organisation – taking account of gender, ethnicity, age, etc. Inclusion means being at the table at all levels of the organisation, being a valued contributor and being fully responsible for your contribution to the ultimate result. Catalyst's report "Inclusive Leadership: The View From Six Countries" (2014) suggests that leaders who wish to create inclusive cultures need to value the diversity of talents, experiences and identities that employees bring. At the same time, they need to find common ground. Focusing too much on the former can lead employees to feel alienated or stereotyped. Focusing primarily on the latter can leave employees reluctant to share views and ideas that might set them apart, increasing the chances of problems like groupthink. When employees feel unique – recognised for their differences – and have a sense of belonging based on sharing common attributes and goals with their peers, organisations best increase the odds of benefiting from workforce diversity. Catalyst's findings suggest that a balanced strategy of meeting employees' needs for uniqueness and belongingness can be more impactful in increasing employee innovation and engagement than a strategy focusing on only one or the other of these needs.

Influencing

A key feature of leadership, performed through communicating, decision-making and motivation. A leader motivates people by creating a desire within them to accomplish things on their own.

Intersectionality
The interconnected nature of social categorisations such as race, class and gender as they apply to a given individual or group, regarded as creating overlapping and interdependent systems of discrimination or disadvantage.

Laissez-faire leadership
Also known as delegative leadership, this is a type of leadership style in which leaders are hands-off and allow group members to make the decisions. Researchers have found that this is generally the leadership style that leads to the lowest productivity among group members.

Leadership
Leadership is both a research area and a practical skill encompassing the ability of an individual or organisation to lead or guide other individuals, teams, or entire organisations. The literature on the subject demonstrates multiple and frequently contrasting viewpoints and approaches about what defines "good leadership".

Leadership development
A professional programme or activity that helps people become better leaders. Leadership development (LD) is normally part of the oganisational development (OD) processes of private and public organisations. It occupies a specific sub-sector in the literature on leadership and has gained a place in most management practice (ranging from executive programmes to tailor-made programmes for individual companies). Programmes vary massively in complexity, cost and contents.

Participative leadership
Also known as the democratic leadership style, this is a method of leadership that involves all team members in identifying important goals as well as developing strategies and procedures to achieve those goals.

Leadership style
A leader's style of providing direction, implementing plans, and motivating people. Multiple authors have proposed numerous different leadership styles as exhibited by leaders in the political, business or other fields – and many style names exist. Just Daniel Goleman alone talks about six styles of leadership, each one springing from different components of emotional intelligence (article "Leadership that Gets Results", 2000). In this glossary a few of the more common ones are referenced.

Management (or managing)
Administration of an organisation, whether it be a business, a not-for-profit organisation, or government body.

Mentoring
A process for an informal transmission of knowledge, social capital, and the psychosocial support perceived by the recipient as relevant to work, career, or professional development. Mentoring entails informal communication, usually face-to-face and over a sustained period of time, between a person who is perceived to have greater relevant knowledge, wisdom, or experience (the mentor) and a person who is perceived to have less (the protégé).

Organisational development
A planned, systematic approach to improving organisational effectiveness – one that aligns strategy, people and processes.

Sponsors
(In this context) mentors advise while sponsors connect, promote and deliver. They make sponsored women visible to leaders within the company, and to top people outside as well. They connect sponsored women to career opportunities and provide "air cover" when they encounter trouble. When it comes to opening doors, they accompany women to the threshold of power.

Transformational leadership
Style of leadership where a leader works with subordinates to identify needed change, creating a vision to guide the change through inspiration, and executing the change in tandem with committed members of a group. Transformational leadership serves to enhance the motivation, morale and job performance of followers through a variety of mechanisms. These include connecting the followers' sense of identity and self to a project and to the collective identity of the organisation; being a role model for followers in order to inspire them and to raise their interest in the project; challenging followers to take greater ownership of their work; and understanding the strengths and weaknesses of followers, allowing the leader to align followers with tasks that enhance their performance.

Sources: Catalyst, UN Women, European Institute for Gender Equality (EIGE), International Labour Organisation (ILO), Mercer and McKinsey. Leadership sources: Harvard Business Review, Oxford University, International Leadership Association and multiple best-selling authors (see Annex I).

NB: Very useful glossaries of gender concepts can be found on the EIGE's website (http://eige.europa.eu/rdc/thesaurus) and on the UN Women website (https://trainingcentre.unwomen.org/mod/glossary/view.php?id=36). EIGE also produces a precious Annual Gender Equality Index for the EU-28 countries (http://eige.europa.eu/rdc/eige-publications).